The People
v.
Tony Blair

Politics, the Media and the
Anti-War Movement

The People
v.
Tony Blair

Politics, the Media and the
Anti-War Movement

Chris Nineham

Winchester, UK
Washington, USA

First published by Zero Books, 2013
Zero Books is an imprint of John Hunt Publishing Ltd., Laurel House, Station Approach,
Alresford, Hants, SO24 9JH, UK
office1@jhpbooks.net
www.johnhuntpublishing.com
www.zero-books.net

For distributor details and how to order please visit the 'Ordering' section on our website.

Text copyright: Chris Nineham 2012

ISBN: 978 1 78099 816 9

A CIP catalogue record for this book is available from the British Library.

Design: Stuart Davies

Printed and bound by CPI Group (UK) Ltd, Croydon, CR0 4YY

We operate a distinctive and ethical publishing philosophy in all
areas of our business, from our global network of authors to
production and worldwide distribution.

CONTENTS

Acknowledgements

This short book is a product of the collective experience I have been lucky enough to share over the last eleven years with a range of talented and committed campaigners in the Stop the War Coalition, some of whom feature in the book. I am very grateful to all of them for many things. The book has drawn on my research at the Communication and Media Research Institute at Westminster University under the guidance of Anthony McNicholas and Pete Goodwin. Their ideas and support have been invaluable. Tariq Goddard's enthusiasm helped convince me to write it. Lindsey German, John Rees, Andrew Murray, Sabah Jawad and Feyzi Ismail have all given me vital ideas or detailed comment for the book or both. Feyzi Ismail's presence in my life made it possible. I hope I have done them all justice.

Introduction

On Tuesday, 11 March 2003, British Defence Secretary Geoff Hoon phoned Donald Rumsfeld, his opposite number in the US, and told him Britain might not participate in the invasion of Iraq. "We in Britain are having political difficulties," he said, "real difficulties, more than you might realise." He explained that there was a real chance an upcoming vote in parliament would go against the war, in which case Britain would have to 'disconnect' its troops from the operation. That night, Donald Rumsfeld went public about Blair's problems at a televised White House press conference, admitting Britain might not be showing up for the invasion. He reassured the media "there are workarounds." Blair, Hoon and their colleagues were furious.[1]

This was nine days before the invasion of Iraq. Hoon's phone call reflected panic in Blair's camp. A few days earlier Home Secretary Jack Straw had told Blair that if he went to war with Bush without a second UN resolution, "the only regime change that will be happening will be in this room."[2] Next day, Jack Straw was apparently one of a number of senior figures arguing with Blair not to join in. In Alistair Campbell's words, "Jack S said that Rumsfeld's idiotic comments gave us a way out."[3] One *Guardian* journalist reported in a piece headlined 'Brought to the brink of defeat,' "Senior civil servants began to check the procedures that might be necessary if Mr Blair was forced to quit."[4]

Whatever Donald Rumsfeld might have meant by 'workarounds' if Britain had pulled out of the war it would have been catastrophic not just for the government but for the whole Iraq operation. As Hoon himself admitted later, the British and US forces were so intertwined there would have been a massive hole in military planning.[5] Worse, the US would have lost vital political cover for an invasion that was leaving it more and more isolated.

The panic in Downing Street was largely a result of public opposition and protest, the impact of what the *New York Times* two days after the 15 February global protests called "the second superpower."[6] That day was the highest point of a movement that Blair admits shocked him and "reminded me of my isolation."[7] It took place at a time of maximum international disarray about the war. As Alistair Campbell noted in his diary the morning of the march, they had both slept badly, "every part of the strategy was in tatters – re the EU, re the UN, re the US, re the party, re the country which was about to march against us."[8]

All this and more has found its way into the public record, at least in the last few years, but it is not in the standard account of the time. The received wisdom is that Blair and his team sailed through those months blithely ignoring all criticism, unimpressed by popular protest and unconcerned by public doubt. Largely of course, this is because he did in the end get away with it; the parliamentary revolt was contained – just – and the war went ahead with all its predicted horror. But it is not just that. Panic and disarray don't fit the 'Teflon Tony' image that has been constructed by Blair and his admirers. More generally the last thing rulers want to do is admit they have been shaken by the action of those they rule. So it should come as no surprise that it is only years after Tony Blair's resignation that the full extent of the crisis caused by opposition to the Iraq war has begun to surface.

Accompanying this crisis was unusual media behaviour. The mainstream media normally ignores, marginalises or even criminalises radical protest. For a short period around the start of the Iraq war something different happened. Not only was there widespread and at times celebratory coverage – including demonstration supplements in the Sunday papers – but some newspapers actively encouraged their readers to participate in demonstrations with maps, arguments and even banner headlines. While the Murdoch press was uniformly hostile and most of the media supported the war, the protests could not be ignored. The *Mirror* took the decision to actively back the anti-war movement. In the run-up to 15 February it regularly carried articles explaining why marching mattered. Senior staff from the *Mirror* actually met with march organisers to discuss how to promote the protest and produced thousands of placards to be distributed on the demonstration itself.

All this reflects the depth of the crisis created by the Iraq war and the movement against it. It is a challenge to the pessimistic view that marching and mass movements change nothing. The Stop the War movement generated not just the biggest demonstrations in British history but also an unprecedented outbreak of direct action, including the biggest wave of school walkouts in British history. In fact the movement broke a series of protest records. 15 February was the biggest protest of all time in Britain and many other countries. Britain's biggest weekday protest took place when 300,000 confronted George Bush on his November 2003 visit to London; and its biggest protest in wartime took place when around half a million marched two days after the bombing started.[9]

As the decade went on the movement also organised further massive demonstrations over Iraq and a series of important marches and protests against the occupation of Afghanistan. In 2006 Stop the War called two very large emergency demonstrations against the Israeli invasion of Lebanon and in 2009 co-organised two massive demonstrations against the Israeli incursions into Gaza. Most important, the real history of the anti-war movement suggests that in fact, co-ordinated mass action does have the power not just to change minds but to challenge governments.

This isn't just a debate about the effectiveness of protest; there are also wider analytical questions at stake. Bush and his coterie were nothing if not self-confident. After a shaky start, 'success' in Afghanistan had the effect of supercharging both Bush and

Blair's sense of mission. Anger at the massive build up of power at the centre of imperialism, the arrogance and cynicism of the Western leaderships, and the more and more obvious links between governments and the corporations can lead to an overestimation of the power of imperialism. Certainly some left-wing analyses of imperialism after the collapse of the Soviet Union reflected Western triumphalism more than real power relations. As we shall see, internal US foreign policy documents from around the turn of the 21st century in fact reveal a mixture of hubris and anxiety, reflecting the US's still dominant but increasingly challenged position in the world. The anti-war protests at the time and in the ten years since the invasion of Iraq have underlined imperialism's vulnerability just as much as its terrible capacity to unleash carnage on the world.

Media behaviour is a constant frustration to those who seek change. Owned and run for the most part by big corporations or governments, the media has a built-in tendency to favour the status quo. This can lead to a sense that the corporate media has a grip on the collective consciousness that can't be loosened. Nick Davies ends his brilliant critique of today's news media *Flat Earth News* with a despairing description of the impact of the corporate media on our future by US radicals John Nichols and Robert McChesney:

> In the place of informed debate or political parties organising along the full spectrum of opinion, there will be vacuous journalism and elections dominated by public relations, big money, moronic political advertising. It is a world where the market and commercial values overwhelm notions of democracy and civic culture, a world where depoliticisation runs rampant, and a world where the wealthy few face fewer and fewer threats of political challenge.[10]

As the tenth anniversary of the invasion of Iraq and the demonstrations comes around, we can assume that normal service has been resumed in the media for the time being, and that the anniversary of the historic protests will largely be ignored. It seemed wrong that the anniversary should pass without these demonstrations and their tremendous impact being re-examined. The aim is to remind ourselves of the sheer criminality of Bush and Blair's conduct, to try and explain what was behind it and how they got away with it, but also to underline, in very dangerous times, the power of mass, popular protest.

Chapter One

The Road to War

"Either Tony knows something the rest of us don't know, or he's insane."

Unnamed government minister, March 2003.[11]

It is not part of the official version of events, but it is a fact that many in George Bush's cabinet saw 9/11 as an opportunity. The word, and others similar, keeps coming up. At the first post-9/11 strategy cabinet, vice president Dick Cheney argued bluntly that events presented them with a chance to strengthen the US position in the Middle East. Deputy Defence Secretary Paul Wolfowitz was equally straightforward. 9/11, he said, "gave the U.S. a window to go after Hussein."[12] A little later, by her own admission, Condoleezza Rice called together senior staff of the National Security Council to discuss "how do you capitalize on these opportunities."[13]

A group of US foreign policy officials and advisors including Donald Rumsfeld, Richard Perle, Richard Armitage, John Bolton and Paul Wolfowitz had been promoting a turn to a much more aggressive foreign policy for years. They were organised around William Kristol's Project for the New American Century (PNAC), they were known as the neo-conservatives, and they were particularly focused on Iraq. Eighteen of them – eleven of whom were to end up serving in the Bush administration – sent a joint letter to the Clinton administration in early 1998 criticising its foreign policy and calling for regime change in Iraq. That same year the Murdoch-owned Kristol-edited neo-conservative house magazine *The Weekly Standard* ran an issue headlined, 'Saddam Must Go – A How to Guide.'[14]

The neo-con tag was first used as a criticism of rightward

moving liberals in the early 1970s. The term was adopted by the group to distinguish their thinking from both the liberal interventionists, who historically tended to rely on the United Nations and international law as vehicles for the propagation of US interests, and the isolationist right who were wary of all foreign adventures. More than anything what defined neo-cons was unilateralism based on the belief that the US was a unique force for good in the world.

Leading neo-con and Bush speech writer David Frum spelt out the logic as it applied to the Iraq adventure:

If the United States overthrew Saddam Hussein next, it could create a reliable American ally in the potential super-power of the Arab world. With American troops so close, the Iranian people would be emboldened to rise against the mullahs. And as Iran and Iraq built moderate, representative pro-Western regimes, the pressure on the Saudis and the other Arab states to liberalize and modernise would intensify.

Their pseudo-democratic dreaming was underpinned with hard power calculation. Frum goes on, "An American-led overthrow of Saddam Hussein would put the US more wholly in charge of the region than any power since the Ottomans, or maybe the Romans."[15]

Whatever the contradictions in their intellectual positions, 9/11 was the neo-cons' moment. Though Rumsfeld and Wolfowitz lost the argument for an immediate attack on Iraq at that first meeting, the opposition was mainly tactical. Bush apparently felt the link with 9/11 was too tenuous for Iraq to be the first target. But no one was against the idea in principle, and as early as 17 September according to the Washington Post, George Bush asked the Pentagon to draft plans for an attack on Iraq.[16]

Emboldened by 'success' in Afghanistan, by the time of the

State of the Union address at the end of January 2002, Bush was talking like a true believer. In the speech he claimed the right to take pre-emptive action against any state perceived as a threat by the US. He listed North Korea, Iraq and Iran as the main enemies in an "Axis of Evil," and the deliberate and deadly confusion between terrorism and "rogue states" was hardwired into his thinking. "The United States of America," he said, "will not permit the world's most dangerous regimes to threaten us with the world's most dangerous weapons."[17] By early spring 2002, minds were well and truly made up. To prove the point, Bush stuck his nose into a spring meeting between Condoleezza Rice and some senators about diplomatic initiatives with Iraq to say simply, "Fuck Saddam, we are taking him out."[18]

Tony Blair was not far behind. Without discussing it in cabinet, as early as the start of March 2002, Tony Blair had commissioned an *Iraq Options* paper from the Overseas and Defence Secretariat of the Cabinet Office outlining options for regime change.[19] He was telling the public and the cabinet that no decisions had yet been taken, but in fact he not only knew that Washington's mind was made up, but he had tied Britain to a war for regime change.

In a top secret memo to Blair dated 14 March 2002, David Manning, the PM's senior advisor on foreign affairs, reported on a dinner meeting with Condoleezza Rice:

> We spent a long time at dinner on Iraq. It is clear that Bush is grateful for your support and has registered that you are getting flak. I said that you would not budge in your support for regime change but you had to manage a press, a Parliament and a public opinion that was very different from anything in the United States.[20]

Days later, British ambassador to the UN Christopher Meyer confirmed Blair had signed up to regime change in Iraq in a meeting with Paul Wolfowitz. "We backed regime change," he reported, "but the plan had to be clever and failure was not an option."[21]

Blair was, then, pursuing an illegal foreign policy behind the backs of parliament and people, let alone his cabinet. His supporters' much-repeated defence was that getting close to Bush was essential to restrain him, to try and ensure there was no action without UN support, and that moves against Iraq would be accompanied by an Israel/Palestine peace initiative. When Blair travelled to the US in April 2002 for a special summit with Bush at his ranch in Crawford, Texas, the Downing Street narrative was that he was going to persuade Bush to work multi-laterally and with a long term plan for Iraq's future.

The reality of the meeting was very different. Before it Blair was indicating to aides that Britain's support for the US was unconditional. "We have always been with the US on this one," he said.[22] American participants including Colin Powell and Bush's chief of staff Andrew Card didn't remember any conditions on British support being tabled at the Crawford encounter, and the Cabinet Office minutes don't mention Blair presenting any strong caveats except that the Americans must help win international opinion for action.[23] David Manning, who was there, was very sceptical too. "I doubt the conditions were that forcibly expressed," he says, "I doubt he even mentioned the UN at Crawford. I don't even remember the UN coming up at Crawford."[24]

Blair spent most of the time at Crawford in one-to-one discussions with the president. At the joint press conference Bush singled out Blair's lack of concern for public opinion for special praise: "History has called us into action. The thing I admire about this prime minister is that he doesn't need a poll or a focus group to convince him of the difference between right and wrong."[25]

The method in their madness

There have been many explanations for the ascendancy of the neo-cons and the resulting mayhem. The neo-cons' rise is often regarded as the result of an aberration, a freak coincidence of a deranged president, a servile media and the overweening power of the oil lobby. John Le Carre brought these themes together eloquently in a January 2003 essay entitled *The United States Has Gone Mad*:

> The combination of compliant US media and vested corporate interests is once more ensuring that a debate that should be ringing out in every square is confined to the loftier columns of the East Coast press... But the American public is not merely being misled. It is being browbeaten and kept in a state of ignorance and fear. The carefully orchestrated neurosis should carry Bush and his fellow conspirators into the next election.[26]

The problem with the view of the war as the outcome of a conspiracy on the US people by a crazed president is that it doesn't explain the broad consensus within US foreign policy circles. While the neo-cons made the running, and there were plenty of tactical and strategic disagreements, what is remarkable is that when the time came, the US foreign policy establishment appears to have been pretty united in supporting the attack with or without UN backing. In the words of Deepa Kumar after 9/11, there was "unanimous agreement in the foreign policy establishment that the War on Terror would henceforth frame US foreign policy."[27]

It also can't explain the fact that, though 9/11 was an important turning point, there was a marked tendency toward interventions over the previous decade, starting with the 1991 attack on Iraq and gathering pace with the wars in Bosnia and Kosovo. In the words of one historian of US foreign policy, "what will stand out one day is not George W Bush's uniqueness but the continuum from the Carter Doctrine to 'shock and awe.'"[28]

Others have stressed the influence of the Zionist lobby on the neo-cons and the wider Washington foreign policy community.[29] There is no doubt that the Israeli lobby is very strong in Washington, but it is not decisive even in ensuring a pro-Israel policy. Unconditional support for Israel spans the political spectrum in Washington foreign policy, across party and religion. From Jeanne Kirkpatrick to Francis Fukuyama and Zalmay Khalilzad, next to no one challenges a militantly pro-Israel policy.

To see the Israeli lobby as a driver of US strategy is to look at the relationship between the US and Israel upside down. The US turned toward the backing of the Israeli state in the late 1960s and 1970s when its traditional allies in the region became unreliable due to the rise of Arab nationalism and later the overthrow of the Shah of Iran. The US backs Israel because it needs a 100% loyal military ally in what the US regards as the most important region of the globe. In fact the idea of a Zionist hold over US foreign policy can help to conceal the real source of the problems in the Middle East. It allows Gulf States to blame Israel and the Zionist lobby for policies that are really made in Washington. It allows them to project the fantasy of influencing the US to taker a tougher line on Israel, and so justifies trying to get close to US policymakers.

Perhaps the most common response at the time was to see the rise of the neo-cons as a product of the unchallenged supremacy of the US worldwide, the achievement of untouchable hyper power status. Hardt and Negris' influential books suggested early last decade that 'empire' had become so powerful and all pervasive that it had transcended national boundaries completely.[30] Other more orthodox commentators have argued the US has been able to maintain an informal empire in the West strong enough for it to launch any attacks it wants with impunity.[31]

Bush was certainly not one to play down US power and its associated responsibilities. In one of his many soaring rhetorical flights at the time he assured us that "Freedom is the Almighty's gift to every man and woman in this world. As the greatest power on earth we have an obligation to help the spread of freedom."[32]

At their most confident, the neo-cons actually felt they and America had a free hand to manufacture global reality. One Bush aide, probably Karl Rove, boasted to a journalist, "We're an empire now, and when we act, we create our own reality. And while you're studying that reality – judiciously, as you will – we'll act again, creating other new realities, which you can study too, and that's how things will sort out. We're history's actors... and you, all of you, will be left to just study what we do."[33]

But the contempt for existing facts on display here suggests a hollowness to the triumphalism. Arrogance and unease mix in equal measure in neo-conservatives' policy statements. The PNAC report written in September 2000 was in effect a warning to the US foreign policy elites:

The United States is the world's only superpower, combining preeminent military power, global technological leadership, and the world's largest economy. Moreover, America stands at the head of a system of alliances that includes the world's other leading democratic powers. At present the United States faces no global rival. America's grand strategy should aim to preserve and extend this advantageous position as far into the future as possible. There are, however, potentially powerful states dissatisfied with the current situation and eager to change it, if they can, in directions that endanger the relatively peaceful, prosperous and free condition the world enjoys today. Up to now, they have been deterred from doing so by the capability and global presence of American military power. But, as that power declines, relatively and absolutely, the happy conditions that follow from it will be inevitably undermined.[34]

"Potentially powerful and dissatisfied states" were the clouds on the horizon of the post-1989 vista. The collapse of communism had swelled the chorus of self-satisfaction celebrating the conquest of neoliberal economic policies domestically under Thatcher and Reagan.

The USSR, the US's main competitor, had been removed from the scene. But the reorganisation of the Western economies along neoliberal lines had itself partly been a response to economic challenges in the sphere of production. The figures speak for themselves: in 1945 the US share of world manufacturing production was around 50%, by 1980 this had dropped drastically to 31%, by the middle of last decade it was down to 25%.[35]

The surpluses that were recycled through Wall Street and increasingly London in the 1980s and 1990s more and more came from production centred abroad, in Taiwan, Singapore, The Pearl River Delta in China and elsewhere.[36] The US boom in the early 1990s helped it to at least temporarily pull Germany and Japan out of economic difficulties, but by the end of the decade the relationship had switched and it was Japan and Germany that were hauling the US out of slowdown.

Meanwhile, by the end of the nineties, it had become clear not just that there was a global slowdown but that, unlike in the period after the Second World War, the US was not able to provide the impetus for growth. Compared to the sluggish performance of most of the Western economies at the time, China's rise was relentless. From 1994 to 2004 its average growth rate was 8.5%.[37] The rise of China was the most serious of a number of threats which the West was worried about.

After the Second World War the US had the economic capacity to pull the Western powers around it and build hegemony across the Western world and direct the struggle against its only serious rival, Russia. Now the US had to face these challenges alone, with much-reduced economic capacity but one massive advantage – huge military preponderance. At the start of the War on Terror the US was responsible for around 33% of the world's total arms spending, significantly higher than the figure during the 1980s. Its 1999 arms expenditure was $281 billion compared to about $88 billion for China, its nearest competitor. US military spending equalled that of the ten countries beneath it on the arms spending league table *taken together*.[38]

Neo-con policy was above all the US's response of choice to this combination of economic decline and military superiority in a more contested world. They would promote Wall Street as a financial centre, continue to use the international financial institutions as a tool to discipline other economies and most importantly increase the use of military power to inhibit the possibility of new economic challengers becoming great powers.

The National Security Strategy document for 2002 is explicit:

We will strongly resist aggression from other great powers – even as we welcome their peaceful pursuit of prosperity, trade and cultural advancement… We are attentive to the possible renewal of old patterns of great power competition. Several potential great powers are now in the midst of internal transition – most importantly Russia, India and China.[39]

Back to the future

Blair's enthusiastic buy-in to the war is often explained in personal terms. Many who saw the Blair-Bush relationship up close noticed how the British prime minister relished being the key ally at the court of King George and he revelled embarrassingly in the ecstatic reception he received at the US Congress when he visited in 2002. He had a reputation too for preferring 'big vision' politics to the banal detail of everyday government.

He liked to be seen as a man with a mission and he admitted to being frustrated with the difficulties of driving through his market-led transformation of public services at home.

But this was not just a matter of temperament. Blair had been developing a radical, interventionist approach to foreign policy for some years. In his memoir he says that 9/11 was the moment he became "a revolutionary," when he understood that the Middle East needed "fundamental re-ordering" and when, in effect, he signed up to the neo-con agenda.[40] Actually Blair had focused on Saddam Hussein in a defining speech he had made on liberal interventionism in Chicago in 1999. The speech contained a generalised argument for more intervention in a more unstable, contested world: "The most pressing foreign policy problem we face is to identify the circumstances in which we should get actively involved in other peoples' conflicts ... the principle of non-interference must be qualified in important respects," but it was also already focusing in on the potential link between terrorism and rogue states.[41]

His developing attitudes drew heavily on the work of his advisor Robert Cooper who argued for the continuing relevance of imperialism in establishing stability, order and progress in an unstable world: "we need to revert to the rougher methods of an earlier era – force, pre-emptive attack, deception, whatever is necessary to deal with those who still live in the 19th century world of every state for itself."[42]

The Kosovo war had been an important moment for Blair. He was the loudest champion of Western intervention against Milosevic, publicly and successfully putting pressure on US President Bill Clinton to take decisive military action. Though the Western bombing of the Serbian forces killed thousands and accelerated the cycle of ethnic cleansing in the region, it was widely presented at the time as a success for the interventionists and Blair took personal credit. In the words of Jeremy Greenstock, UK ambassador to the UN at the time, "He felt that his determination, his sense of mission in that occasion had been vindicated."[43]

Blair was then, by 9/11, as much a neo-con in foreign policy terms as any in Washington. He was jealous in fact of the enthusiastic interventionism of the US Congress and confided in an aide that he wished Britain's parliamentarians "would be so eager to do the right thing."[44]

But Blair's personal journey alone can't explain Britain's participation. The fact of the matter was, that despite controversy in the British establishment over the war, Blair was far from alone, and elite opposition to his plans was half-baked. Britain's involvement was in the end the logical outcome of its orientation on the special relationship with the United States that Blair regarded as "a matter of faith" and to which the British political classes are almost universally signed up. Once the world's leading colonial power, Britain retains a level of foreign investment and assets unique in Europe. It has the highest investment in the US and has cultural, historical linguistic links with that country. Its alliance with the US in the Second World War corresponded with the demise of its empire but gave birth to a subordinate relationship that the whole of the British ruling class regards not just as beneficial, but as the centrepiece of foreign policy. This relationship has been further strengthened by the transatlantic championing of neoliberalism begun in the days of the Thatcher-Reagan love-in.

US unilateralism over Iraq presented the British establishment with a dilemma. But left to its own devices its choice was never really in doubt. There was of course the danger of isolation in Europe, but the calculation was the Europeans would probably come around to supporting the war once they realised they couldn't stop it, a gamble which turned out to be correct. Even those who had doubts knew that breaking from Bush over Iraq would mean a complete recasting of British foreign policy, something for which they were personally and politically completely unprepared.

Impact on public opinion caused more concern than any matters of principle or worries about the likely consequences of a war. There was real anxiety about reaction in the Labour party and amongst the wider public, who hated what Bush stood for and were taking to the streets in huge numbers. In Alistair Campbell's words, "My big worry was his political position vis-à-vis what would be an unpopular war alongside a very right-wing American president. I was worried how it might affect his survival."[45] Still, most in the cabinet stayed quiet, at least in public. Blair survived. But he, his party and the British establishment are still dealing with the damage caused.

Chapter Two

A Hard Sell

"With a heavy dose of fear and violence, and a lot of money for projects, I think we can convince these people that we are here to help them."
Lt. Col. Nathan Sassaman, battalion commander in Abu Hishma, Iraq, 2003.[46]

It's widely acknowledged that governments leverage wars to increase power over their populations. Sixteenth century philosopher Erasmus noted that "once war has been declared, then all the affairs of state are at the mercy of the appetites of a few."[47] The suspension of popular liberties has indeed been a part of wartime experience. Left commentators tend particularly to stress the dire ideological effects of going to war:

> When the huge news outlets swing behind warfare, the dissent propelled by conscience is not deemed to be very newsworthy. The mass media are filled with bright lights and sizzle, with high production values and lower human values, boosting the war effort. And for many Americans, the gap between what they believe and what is on their TV sets is the distance between their truer selves and their fearful passivity.[48]

Such pessimism is hardly surprising given the abysmal record of modern media in wartime. All the evidence shows that the limited level of media independence from power that exists in 'normal times' goes up in smoke the day hostilities start.[49] Some journalists admit this without shame. For Max Hastings, *Evening Standard* Falklands war correspondent in 1982, and now with the

Daily Mail, "no British reporter could be neutral when his own country was fighting: objectivity was a peacetime luxury, and reporting became an extension of the war effort."[50]

But the historical record is complicated. While governments routinely use wars to concentrate power, stir up nationalism and racism and curb civil liberties, the hypocrisy, dislocation, suffering and sacrifice involved tends to lead at some point to discontent. The 20th century is littered with examples of social turmoil generated by war. Tom Wells' history of the impact of the Vietnam War in the US describes how opposition to the war and reaction to the secret bombing of Cambodia in 1970 shook American society to its core:

> To many Americans, the domestic uproar following Cambodia... suggested that the country was becoming unhinged. Newspapers observed that the United States was as divided as it had been since the Civil War. The country was on the verge of a 'physical breakdown,' commented New York's Mayor John Lindsay. 'The nation disintegrates,' lamented John Gardner, the Johnson administration's Secretary of Home Affairs. 'I use the phrase soberly: the nation disintegrates.' McGeorge Bundy, one of the war's main architects, who was now president of the Ford Foundation, declared: 'Not only must there be no new incursion of Americans across the Cambodian frontier, but nothing that feels like that to the American public must ever happen again... Any major action of this general sort... would tear the administration and the country to pieces... The chances of general domestic upheaval would be real.'[51]

In the case of Iraq, there was a marked contrast between the confidence of the war makers in their countries' global mission and their success in creating enthusiasm for war at home and abroad. Though the attack on Afghanistan was popular in the

US, war fever failed to materialise over Iraq, despite stereotypes of an ignorant and brainwashed population. Though on some calculations a majority in the US backed action on Iraq, as late as January 2003 two thirds of Americans wanted Bush to wait till the UN inspectors did their job rather than attack immediately, and favoured a diplomatic solution.[52] In Britain there was majority opposition to the war from summer 2002 onwards, growing to 80% and even 90% of the population in early 2003 according to some polls, before dropping dramatically for a few months. In both countries opposition grew steadily again a few months after the war began.

The Empire problem

Grasping the dynamic behind the War on Terror helps us understand Bush and Blair's problems.

Imperialism has always posed certain ideological difficulties for the US. At the moment of US supremacy post-Second World War, anti-colonial struggles had delegitimated naked intervention and the kind of openly racist ideas that had traditionally underpinned European colonialism. The UN Declaration of Human Rights disavowed racism and based international relations on the rhetoric of universal rights. The US achieved hegemony in the post-war world partly by posing as the opponent of the old colonial blocs and depicting itself as the pinnacle of civilisation and a champion of decolonisation and development. But this ideology often came into conflict with the US's real policy of informal empire that was often backed up by the use of force, most spectacularly over Vietnam.

The Cold War provided a partial solution. It was a struggle for influence and control in key regions of the globe with Russia, the US's main competitor at the time. The output of the Russian economy grew from 33% of that of the US in 1950 to just under 60% by the 1970s. Productivity in Russia nearly caught up with that of European countries by 1980.[53] But this was a death struggle that could be dressed up in ideological clothes. Freedom was conflated with free markets and the struggle against 'totalitarianism' was used to justify interventions bolstering US influence in the post-colonial world.

Economies flowing from the greater size of the US and its ability to reach into global markets ensured the US victory in that defining post-war struggle.[54] The brief triumphalism that followed the collapse of communism at the start of the 1990s created a sense of the inevitability of the spread of US power and influence, most imaginatively packaged in Francis Fukuyama's famous but premature book *The End of History*.

But as we have seen, in reality, US elites had become anxious that during the period of the post-war informal empire, other economic powers had been able to develop under the military protection of the West without actually having to waste much money on arms. This is the secret to the growing differences in approach between the US and 'Old Europe' and to the resentments created by opposition to the Iraq War there. As foreign affairs commentator and PNAC signatory Robert Kagan put it in 2003:

> The current situation abounds in ironies. Europe's rejection of power politics and its devaluing of military force as a tool of international relations have depended on the presence of American military forces on European soil. Europe's new Kantian order could flourish only under the umbrella of military power exercised according to the old Hobbesian order. American power made it possible for Europeans to believe power is no longer important.[55]

Neo-conservatism was precisely a critique of the 'end of history' delusion insofar as it translated into a reliance on dominance through the benign spread of the free market or luxuriated in a peace dividend. The 2000 PNAC report was explicit:

Preserving the desirable strategic situation in which the United States now finds itself requires a globally preeminent military capability both today and in the future. But years of cuts in defense spending have eroded the American military's combat readiness, and put in jeopardy the Pentagon's plans for maintaining military superiority in the years ahead... Without a well-conceived defense policy and an appropriate increase in defense spending, the United States has been letting its ability to take full advantage of the remarkable strategic opportunity at hand slip away.[56]

In the wake of the end of the Cold War there was a question mark about how such policies of increased intervention could be packaged. One option was to resort to racism. Harvard academic Samuel Huntingdon was the single most influential proponent of the notion that the Muslim world was inherently destabilising and a barrier to the spread of 'civilised' Western values. His 1993 book *The Clash of Civilizations* gained widespread support on the right and its themes have been echoed by sections of the liberal left.

The spread of Islamophobia has been closely connected to the growing intervention in the Middle East. The endless stream of caricature and demonisation of Muslims is usually framed in terms of Muslims' alleged propensity to violence, their hostility to the modern values of democracy and pluralism, even their tendency to want to spread Islam forcibly if possible. All themes that provide useful cover for the West's imperial ambitions.[57] These stereotypes are so common in the public realm, and their links to the War on Terror so obvious, that they have encouraged the view that the West's recent wars do indeed amount to a clash of Western civilisation with the Muslim world, whereas in fact neo-con policy documents are written in the chilling but clinical jargon of pure power politics.

Islamophobia has great advantages as a means of justifying

modern wars. Although in reality it is a form of racism, it often presents itself as cultural critique. It has thus enabled a host of intellectuals who would not use openly racist language to roll up their sleeves and join in the denunciation of Islam as the centrepiece of a wider, supposedly progressive assault on the backwardness of religion. Another advantage is that it can be used to introduce harsh restrictions on civil liberties at home. As Liz Fekete has pointed out, the parallels with McCarthyism can hardly be ignored:

> As Islamism replaces communism as the new totalitarianism against which we are urged to unite, the 'Islam Scare' supplants the 'red scare'. While the 'reds' were potentially allied to the evil Soviet Empire, Muslims may be secretly allying themselves to an equally evil and totalitarian fundamentalist empire: the *Umma* of global Islam... For just as the 'red scare' was used to argue that traditional security methods could not adequately safeguard the US against the communist threat, the 'Islam scare' now holds that certain beliefs are so dangerous that any measure to restrict them is justified.[58]

That Islamophobia has had a toxic effect on Western societies since 9/11 is borne out by statistics of police and security services' harassment of Muslims, and the prevalence of vicious attacks on Muslims by the media and politicians.[59] But the strong 'clash of civilisations' version has certain drawbacks for the warmakers, the most important being that it is too blunt an instrument with which to carve a justification for a complex policy in the Middle East. In reality some of the most reactionary religious regimes are counted amongst the US's key allies in the Middle East and so messaging the war simply as a battle with Islam is untenable. But Islamophobia remains important background noise, useful in creating an atmosphere in which wars against Muslim countries can be waged. What has emerged in particular is a good Muslim/bad Muslim distinction which focuses on militant radical groups but can be used to frighten mainstream organisations away from taking political positions, and still carries with it the implication that there is something benighted about the religion as a whole.

Islamophobic attitudes coloured Western leaders' response to the 9/11 attacks from the start. 9/11 served as justification for military action in Afghanistan for a time. The invasion initially secured relatively high approval rates because it came so soon after 9/11 and because it was presented as a justified response. This of course was far from the truth. None of the perpetrators of 9/11 came from the country and the war was against the Taliban, not Al-Qaeda. The war in Afghanistan has been a disaster even when judged in the narrow terms of whether it has made the world a safer place. There is plenty of evidence that the US passed on an opportunity to bring Osama Bin Laden to justice in their rush to war.[60] And it is unarguable that Al-Qaeda has spread since then across a wide crescent that stretches from Pakistan to Somalia.

Tell me lies about Iraq

The post-9/11 effect didn't extend to the question of invading Iraq. Attempts to connect Iraq with Al-Qaeda in the popular imagination had some temporary success in the US – some polls showed a majority briefly believed that Iraq was responsible for 9/11 – but this claim was too far-fetched for even the largely eager-to-please US media to sustain for long. This is why the attempt had to be made to portray Saddam's regime as exceptionally oppressive of his own people and dangerous for the region and beyond. The focus was on the claim that Saddam had 'weapons of mass destruction,' chemical, biological or other, which could be used at home or abroad. Given Western support for regimes that were more despotic than Saddam's and more closely linked to radical Islam, and that weapons inspectors were reporting less and less evidence of WMD and more and more co-operation with the regime, this was a tall order.[61]

However, the effort was duly made. The biggest single initiative was the *Iraq Dossier* produced by the British government on 25 September 2002 and based – loosely as it turned out – on British intelligence reports. Two particular claims in the dossier turned out to be deliberate lies. The first was that Iraq had been involved in sourcing illegal uranium from Africa in order to produce nuclear weapons. The International Atomic Energy Agency itself went public in March 2003 to say that the documents on which this claim was based were "obvious fakes."[62]

The second was the assertion that Saddam Hussein had weapons of mass destruction that could be readied for use in 45 minutes. The document's introduction, written by Tony Blair, highlighted the claim: "the document discloses that his [Saddam's] military planning allows for some of the WMD to be ready within 45 minutes of an order to use them."[63]

The truth was not just that the so-called intelligence was dubious at best, but that ministers deliberately distorted it in order to make the case for war. BBC journalist Andrew Gilligan was vilified and later sacked for making this exact claim in a *Today Programme* report in May 2003. BBC Director General Greg Dyke was scandalously forced to resign over the issue in early 2004. Although the conclusions of the Hutton Inquiry in 2004 tried to exonerate Blair and the government, the real picture has subsequently become clear.

Even the government later admitted their information was unreliable. In October 2004 Jack Straw conceded that the sources for the 45-minute claim had "come into question." Five years later, according to the *Guardian*, information had come to light that the source of the claim was a taxi driver on the Iraqi-Jordanian border "who had remembered an overheard conversation in the back of his cab a full two years earlier."[64]

On 12 May 2011, the *Guardian* reported that one of those involved in writing the dossier, Major General Michael Laurie, wrote to the Chilcot Inquiry in 2011 saying, "the purpose of the dossier was precisely to make a case for war, rather than setting out the available intelligence, and that to make the best out of sparse and inconclusive intelligence the wording was developed with care." And on 26 June 2011, the *Guardian* reported on a memo from John Scarlett to Blair's foreign affairs adviser, released under the Freedom of Information Act, which referred to "the benefit of obscuring the fact that in terms of WMD Iraq is not that exceptional."

At the Chilcot Inquiry one of Blair's lines of defence was that the dossier was a non-event at the time, gaining significance only in retrospect. This was fabrication. Parliament was in fact recalled to hear Blair's report on the dossier for one of only three times in the last decade, the other two being for 9/11 and the death of the Queen mother. The 45-minute claim became the basis for a series of sensational newspaper headlines including the infamous *Sun* splash 'Brits 45 Mins from Doom' and the *Evening Standard*'s '45 Minutes from Attack.'[65] The day after the dossier's release national newspapers carried more than 100 separate stories mentioning weapons of mass destruction.

The dossier was used as the centrepiece for Blair's own oft-repeated arguments in parliament and elsewhere that Saddam was a proven threat to the region, an argument that many felt swung the balance of opinion in parliament.

But while Blair and his friends did enough to convince some MPs and the more gung-ho newspaper editors, their efforts had little impact on public opinion. Days after the release of the dossier 350,000 people marched against the war in London on what was, at the time, Britain's biggest ever anti-war march. Strengthened by this massive movement, opinion continued to harden against the war. Many people had clearly made up their mind that Tony Blair had made up his months before, and for the wrong reasons. Particularly as the government refused to discuss the provenance of the intelligence in order to "protect sources," the dossier looked like what it was: a rather desperate effort to justify the unjustifiable.

The most comprehensive survey of the global demonstrations on 15 February noted, "the one opinion shared by almost all the participants in the demonstrations is that the United States wants to invade Iraq to secure its oil supply."[66] Because of their poorly-concealed aggression, their isolation, their attempts at secret collaboration, their generally pro-business agenda and the weakness of their arguments, a huge number of people had rightly drawn the conclusion that Bush and Blair were pursuing their own imperialist agendas in Iraq.

When war broke out, some wavered and were prepared to give the warmakers the benefit of the doubt. But by the autumn of 2003 it had become clear that Saddam's WMD existed only in the overheated imaginations of those with a stake in the war. British opinion turned decisively against the war again, this time for good.

The only argument left was the one about democracy. We have seen that part of the neo-con dogma is that removing dictators by overwhelming force 'frees up' societies for the market and spreads democracy. Previous US leaders were more sceptical. Reagan ran 'democracy enhancement' programmes to back up his interventions particularly in Central America. In fact he tended to run two. He knew the problem was that in elections the wrong person might win, so he ran one programme to set up apparently credible elections, and another to make sure their man won.[67]

In the case of Iraq there was little preparation, little planning for post-occupation and not much money to buy up loyal political elites or placate a traumatised population. The Iraqi people felt the terrifying force of Western-style shock and awe and then were expected in good neo-con fashion to embrace Western-style asset-stripping and privatisation with gratitude. No wonder then that the occupiers quickly dropped discussion about democracy.

In June 2003, the invaders started cancelling promised elections in Iraq. According to the office of Paul Bremer, head of the Coalition Provisional Authority in Iraq – colonial governor effectively – "The most organised political groups in many areas are rejectionists, extremists and remnants of the Ba'athists, they have an advantage over the other groups."[68] A few months later Bremer imposed a series of decrees that included "the full privatisation of public enterprises, full ownership rights by foreign firms of Iraqi businesses, full repatriation of foreign profits... and the elimination of nearly all trade barriers."[69] Elections would have to wait for the real business of the occupation – economic takeover by force.

At the height of its power after the Second World War the US had been able to back up its firepower with soft power, loans and aid, which had bound the West to it and helped to extend its influence in important parts of the developing world. Now, in the heat of war, the democratic veneer burnt off the neo-conservative project and we were left with its essence: brute force.

David Armstrong's celebrated 2002 expose of neo-conservative 'thinking' had been horribly vindicated:

The Plan is for the United States to rule the world. The overt theme is unilateralism, but it is ultimately a story of domination. It calls for the United States to maintain its overwhelming military superiority and prevent new rivals from rising up to challenge it on the world stage. It calls for dominion over friends and enemies alike. It says not that the United States must be more powerful, or most powerful, but that it must be absolutely powerful.[70]

Chapter Three

The Second Superpower

"There may still be two superpowers on the planet: the United States and world public opinion." New York Times, 17 February 2003.[71]

The global demonstrations on 15 February 2003 were the biggest protest event in world history. No one has been able to come up with anything like a historical precedent. Researchers estimate there were demonstrations in at least 800 cities around the world and that anywhere between eight and thirty million marched.[72] The protests unfolded around the globe in sync with the sun. Waking on the Saturday morning activists in Britain learnt that Australia had already had its largest ever protests – four demonstrations of more than 100,000 including between 300,000 and 500,000 in Sydney. Around a million Australians marched in all, about 5% of the entire population.[73]

That set a pattern. Not only was this a genuinely worldwide day of mass action but, though there was marked unevenness, country after country had their biggest protest in generations, or ever. Many of the biggest demonstrations were in Europe. Organisers in Rome estimated three million marched. In Madrid the movement claimed 1.5 million and there were massive marches in other Spanish cities. 45,000 people marched in Switzerland, its biggest demonstration since 1945. More than 100,000 marched in Norway in all – making it the biggest protest since 1917.[74]

But there were significant demonstrations in every region of the globe with the exception, apparently, of China. The biggest demonstration in the Middle East was in Damascus, where US broadcaster CBS estimated 200,000 marched, but there were protests across the region, including a co-ordinated demonstration in Tel Aviv and Ramallah.[75] On the day, the Egyptian movement held a small illegal protest, but they were inspired by the global marches to call a breakthrough protest a few weeks later, which marked the re-emergence of popular protest in the country.

This illustrated another characteristic of 15 February. The scale and momentum behind the day gave activists living in authoritarian regimes the confidence to take to the streets. Around 3,000 people braved their way to the US embassy in Kuala Lumpur on an illegal demonstration the police had promised to attack. In Jordan 5,000 protested and in Tunisia 2,000 demonstrators faced down attacks by armed riot police.

Elsewhere, leading ANC figures joined the tens of thousands marching in South Africa. In Antarctica a group of scientists at the US McMurdo Station held a rally on the ice at the edge of the Ross Sea.[76] In the US hundreds of thousands marched in New York and clashed with police who tried and failed to stop what was supposed to be a static protest turning into a march. Desmond Tutu and Susan Sarandon addressed the rally, amongst others. Major US cities all had big marches. In Seattle organisers had expected 20,000 or 30,000 and were amazed when over 50,000 people turned up, more than at the WTO protests four years before.[77] In Los Angeles 50 or 60,000 joined Martin Sheen and Mike Farrell and director Rob Reiner to march down Hollywood Boulevard.[78] In South America the biggest demonstrations were in Uruguay and Argentina, but there were protests across the continent, including at least 20 in Brazil, in one of which President Lula Da Silva joined in.[79]

Organisers reported higher than expected turnouts even when protests were organised in the last few days. The Uruguay demonstration was organised by a group of anti-capitalists after they heard about the day at the World Social Forum in Brazil two weeks before. On the day some 50,000 marched through the capital city of Montevideo. This is in a country of a little over three million.

London was one of the centres of the action. Britain had had the first great anti-Iraq War demonstration in September 2002 when 350,000 marched. It was activists from Britain who had first proposed the international day, quickly winning support from members of the Italian movement, and then agreement across Europe. Leading US campaigners Jesse Jackson and Tim Robbins came over especially to march in London, because they shared the understanding that the British government was the most vulnerable point of the war effort. Blair was clearly at odds with the British people and his own party. If the US's main ally could be dislodged there was just a chance the whole project could collapse.

The epic proportions of the upcoming demonstration started to sink in on the day, about two weeks before the march, that coach numbers reached 1,000. The take-up was boosted further by a clumsy government attempt to stop the march. With contempt for both public opinion and civil liberties that was typical of New Labour, Culture Secretary Tessa Jowell refused to sign off on the demo route claiming the Hyde Park authorities were worried about damage to the park's grass. This transparent ploy caused outrage. The Stop the War Coalition took a strong public stand, said the march was going ahead whatever happened and suggested Buckingham Palace as an alternative end point. Desperately trying to save face, the Hyde Park author-ities raised health and safety issues: numbers of people; the depth of winter; the dark, poorly lit park; unsafe, muddy ground and so on; but the damage was done. In the face of popular rage and ridicule Tessa Jowell and her park keeper allies backed down humiliated.

It became clear the original meet up point on the Thames Embankment was going to be overrun, so a second meet up point was organised a mile south of Euston Station. On the day enormous crowds amassed there too. People travelling down on the trains from the north to Euston found the crowds had backed up from New Oxford Street way past the Euston Station entrance. Some waited four hours before they even started walking. Incredibly the two marches synchronised and met at a euphoric moment in Piccadilly Circus, right by the statue of Eros.

The demonstration morphed into a wave of humanity moving east-west across central London. Thousands confronted police in Oxford Street, a mile away from the official route, and the police had to stand down, overwhelmed. London belonged to the people that day and no one had experienced anything quite like it. There were still thousands of people pouring into the Hyde Park endpoint and chanting, an hour after the speeches had ended and the sun had gone down.

To savour the moment people lit fires around the park and partied into the evening.

As ever there was debate about the actual size of the demonstration, with the police particularly reluctant to accept that a million marched. Most of the media, however, didn't even try to call it less. Up to now no one has developed an authoritative way of calculating these kind of numbers on the move, but the best research suggests a figure of around two million. The *Guardian* reported an ICM poll taken the day after the demonstration, which concluded that, "at least one person from 1.25 million households in Britain went on Saturday's anti-war march in London."

Given that more than one person must have attended from many households, two million seems to be the best estimate. A *Telegraph* poll came up with a similar figure.[81]

After its size, it was the diversity of the protesters that stood out. As on the previous Stop the War demos, the Muslim communities were out in force alongside the left and the trade unions. But the demonstration's power was that it brought together so many sections of society. There were celebrities including Kylie

Minogue, Damon Albarn and boxer Chris Eubank driving a truck rigged up with the slogan 'Reason should be our only weapon.' There were Labour Party delegations alongside the unions, huge student contingents, Lib Dem supporters, a big turnout from the peace movement, Christian and Buddhist and Jewish groups, and thousands and thousands of first-time marchers who earned the new tag, 'protest virgins.'

The unity of purpose, the sheer size and the long wait combined to break down barriers. One first timer noted, "rookie marchers stood with the Save the Lentil brigade and talked Iraq, Zoe Ball, Greenham Common and bladder control. The smell of Chanel No. 5 mingled with the aroma of cannabis. At Westminster there was a mass stop off at McDonalds. I spotted a Liberty Scarf, a National Trust umbrella and a little blue Tiffany Shop bag."[82]

Graphic artist David Gentleman had urged Stop the War to produce a simple poster and placard that could be carried on the demonstration to express the movement's message clearly and crisply. He came up with the brilliant 'NO' sign that was carried by tens of thousands on the day alongside many produced by the *Mirror*. But as in all genuinely popular movements many carried homemade banners including the later to be mass-produced 'Make tea not war,' one from Shoreham-by-Sea Twins Group, another carried by devotees of East Anglian hardcore metal, and one brought by gardeners announcing 'Gardeners dig peace.'

With the exception of the Murdoch press, the newspapers couldn't miss the message. This, they agreed, with various degrees of enthusiasm or distaste, was definitely not the usual suspects. Some journalists were alarmed, not just by the demographic, but by the universal anger and militancy on display. The *Daily Mail*'s Robert Hardman wrote of "Barbours and burqas, monks and mullahs, Tories and Trots... 'George Bush – terrorist! Tony Blair – terrorist!' they chorused as they marched down Piccadilly. The last time I had heard anyone shouting that it was an angry mob in Pakistan. Now the same mantra was being chanted by Middle England outside Fortnum and Mason."

The interviews, the surveys, the speeches and the reports testify to a mix of emotions amongst the demonstrators on the day, including real fear of the consequences of war and a sense of awe and pride that so many people had turned out to oppose it. But what was noticeable above all was distrust of the warmakers' arguments. Virgin marcher Mike Shaw summed up a widespread cynicism about what was driving the rush to war:

> This is the first time in my life I have ever felt strongly enough about something to come out and protest. Nobody we know supports this war. Containment would work especially with the inspection regime in place at the moment. [Weapons of mass destruction] can't be the reason for all this. I think it has been part of Bush's agenda from the moment he came to power. They want to impose their own systems of government...[83]

Behind this there was a more general feeling of betrayal directed against the politicians who had got us to this point and particularly focused on Tony Blair. In the words of *Guardian* journalist Richard Williams:

> Whatever else it may have been, the march was a great shout of protest against a man for whom most of those present had voted in the last two general elections. After the long alienating years of Thatcher, Tony Blair presented himself as one of us, part of the culture of modern Britain. But now one piece of foreign policy has provided the catalyst for the release of pent-up disenchantment.[84]

From the stage, speaker after speaker expressed this sense of disillusion. Mark Serwotka talked of the social cost of the war: "This war will cost £3.5 billion of our money. Why can't that money be used to fund decent pensions, the health service, pay our fire fighters a decent wage?" Singer Ms Dynamite talked of her belief in the equality of all humanity "which clashes so strongly with the values of the prime minister... We are standing, we are speaking out, we are fighting, but our prime minister is ignoring our wishes."

The demonstration was so vast and the gulf between the people and the politicians so wide that many began to draw more general conclusions from the day. In the words of Madeline Bunting:

Saturday proved that the decline of democracy has been overstated. What has changed is the pattern of participation: political parties and turnouts may be declining, but intense, episodic political engagement is on the increase. In recent years we have seen both the lowest turnouts and the biggest demonstrations in British political history. Now there is a conundrum to keep hundreds of political scientists busy.[85]

The meaning of the march

The evidence backs up Bunting's views. And it makes surprising reading for anyone who thinks that people have become apathetic or depoliticised in the last few decades. The best research into the day's events confirms the diversity of the demonstration – a very wide social, age and gender spectrum participated, "every group in society was represented to some extent", though it was "somewhat younger, slightly more female and especially much better educated than the average citizen." A narrow majority, (54%) were women, 11% were under 24 and another 11% over 65, with the largest percentage in the 45-64 age range (39%), narrowly ahead of the 25-44 group (38%). According to these figures managers made up 6% of the demonstrators and office and manual workers together 20%. Another 20% of the respondents were students.

Though it was diverse, it was not simply a cross section of society. The survey's authors conclude that the protesters fitted the profile of the new social movements more closely than that of the population as a whole. They also find that the movement concentrated its attractive power in general on those with broadly left-wing views.[86] It also records a very high level of people who have demonstrated previously, suggesting 45% of demonstrators had previously been on a peace protest, 27% on a protest over social issues, and 25% against racism.[87]

The anti-war movement was part of, and an accelerator in, a wider, global, trend towards involvement in street protest. Since the early 1970s, a growing percentage of the UK population has reported taking part in demonstrations or other political activism. An examination of the British Social Attitudes surveys over the three decades to 2003 shows an uneven but dramatic rise in the number of people who say they have demonstrated against the government some time in their life. In 1983 the figure was 2% of the population, it then peaked at 12% in 2003.[88] A similar, if slightly less marked trend is apparent in the World Values Survey which also shows a steady rise in the number of people saying they have participated in demonstrations over the same period.[89]

In 2005, 6.4% of the British population confirmed participating in a demonstration in the last five years.[90] If this is correct it would mean in the first five years of the new millennium almost three million people in this country demonstrated. Over a third of these – 1.2 million – were aged between 12 and 25.

The trend towards political street protesting has coincided with a sharp lowering in the public's confidence in core institutions of political society and particularly in the relevance of the political process. The British Social Attitudes Survey records a relatively steady increase in the number of people saying that they "almost never" trust the British government to place the national interest above the interests of their own political party from 10% in 1974 to 30% in 2003.[91]

The same surveys reveal a steep drop in the number of people who believe that there is "a good deal of difference" between political parties, from 80% in 1987 to 15% in 2003 and just 12% in 2005.[92]

Not surprisingly there has at the same time been a steep decline in membership of political parties. In 1983 just under 4% of the British population were members of the main political parties. This figure dropped sharply to 2% in the early 1990s, rose slightly around the 1997 election and then fell again dramatically to just over 1% in 2005, with Labour leading the fall.[93] This decline in political engagement is part at least of a European and almost certainly an international trend. But in Pippa Norris' study of what she calls a "global democratic deficit," the UK Parliament comes out worst in a Europe-wide survey of trust in parliamentary institutions.[94]

It has also coincided with a steep increase in the number of people who self define as left-wing.

The percentage of British people who position themselves on the left has grown in size across all age groups. One recent summary of polling information calculated that it means that the 'left' consists of over seven million people, up from 4.8 million in 1981. The most striking change is amongst the young. The percentage of 15 to 29-year-olds who identify themselves as left-wing has grown from 12% in 1981 to 20% in 2006. When translated into actual numbers it means almost 2.5 million young people define themselves as on the left, with about 750,000 placing themselves on the far left.[95]

The Stop the War campaign has not just reflected this trend, it has helped create it. In the words of convenor Lindsey German:

These demos were of an absolutely unique scale in Britain and of course they had a big impact. Far from it being the case that they have led people to think demonstrations don't work, actually, demonstrations have entered popular culture in the last decade. If you look at all sorts of TV programmes and soaps it's common for people to get out the placards and go on the streets. This reflects the reality. There is much more of a sense that you can't rely on politicians. It's encouraged the idea that you can demonstrate over all sorts of things.[96]

15 February was not, then, just an outburst over a single issue. It expressed outrage at the government's war policies but it also had a wider significance. The movement crystallised a general sense that parliament was not representing the people and that politicians' priorities had been hijacked. It was a high point in a trend towards protest politics that reflects not a depoliticisation of society but a sense of the possibilities of people power. It was part of a process of popular radicalisation.

Chapter Four

The Making of a Movement

"If they start a war we must stop the country."
Report of the Peoples' Assembly, 12 March 2003.

The movement against the Iraq War drew on the experience and energy of the anti-capitalist movement that had produced massive protests against corporate power at meetings at the WTO and the G8 conferences. The Battle of Seattle at the 1999 WTO ministerial meeting had sent a signal around the world that it was possible to organise against the neoliberals even in the heartlands of dotcom capitalism. The July 2001 protests at the Genoa G8 were a formative experience for a generation of activists in Europe. After days of direct action in which the young activist Carlo Giuliani had been shot dead by the police, 300,000 people marched through the sweltering streets of Genoa demanding an end to the radical irresponsibility of the new masters of the neoliberal universe. When 9/11 came just three months later, there was widespread opposition to everything Bush and his supporters stood for, and the movement had experienced mass mobilisations on a scale not seen for a generation.

One of the remarkable things about the anti-capitalist movement was the fact that it had fused massive mobilisations with radical, generalised politics, forcing anyone who was paying attention to at least modify the traditional left dogma that popular campaigns can only be mobilised around single issues. The anti-war movement inherited this approach. In the words of one of its founder members, John Rees:

Although nominally about a single issue it was in fact a broad critique of the economic and political imperatives of the new imperialism. The corporate backers of war, the economics of the oil industry, the environmental impact of war, the working of the military-industrial complex, the fate of Palestine, opposition to the oppression of Muslims, the traditional concerns of anti-nuclear campaigners, the history of Western colonialism all fitted easily into the anti-war movement, deepening rather than narrowing its appeal.[97]

None of this means the anti-war movement was spontaneous. The attack on the Twin Towers and the Pentagon on 11 September 2001 generated shock and anxiety in equal measure. The right were obviously going to try and take the initiative. But the response from the left was very varied. In the US, the anti-globalisation movement was thrown off balance by the attacks and intimidated by the government's attempt to whip up xenophobia. Its planned protests against the IMF in September 2002 bore no comparison to the mass mobilisation against the WTO at Seattle in 1999. Even by the time of the Iraq invasion many countries hadn't organised an effective anti-war network, a fact that provides the main explanation for the unevenness in the demonstrations on 15 February.

A fast and decisive response to 9/11 from the left and the movement was critical. In the words of one of the Muslim activists involved in Britain, Shaheda Vawda:

Everyone had the same sense of urgency. This event had clearly changed the world. It felt to all of us as if we were on the precipice of something quite momentous, and that things could go horribly wrong.[98]

In Britain in the days after 9/11 a group of socialists resolved to call the biggest possible rally as a response to the attacks. There had been at least one socialist meeting about the events. This had to be something different. The plan was to make it as large as possible and involve the widest possible forces. Again, in the words of John Rees:

> Left-wing meetings are fine and important. But if you are going to go up against the US state you better make sure you have the widest possible panoply of forces involved. The biggest possible hall was booked and the most high profile speakers approached. The elements that would go on to form the backbone of the movement – the peace movement, trade unionists, Muslim organisations, anti-capitalist networks – were all contacted.[99]

The success of rally, billed as 'Stop the War before it Starts' surprised everyone, including MP Jeremy Corbyn who was one of the speakers:

> The place was absolutely heaving with people. I had trouble getting in. By the time I had struggled through the crowds into the main hall there had been a change of plan. A number of us were sent out around the building to speak at overflow meetings. I spoke at all of them, so by the time I got onto the main stage and made my speech there, it was the third time I had spoken. Then I was sent outside and climbed onto a wall by a bus stop to speak to several hundred people outside the building. Even the people waiting at the bus stop listened. I was overjoyed that so many people had come out to show their concern.[100]

This was the launch of the Stop the War Coalition, formalised at another mass meeting a week later. Bringing the elements of the movement together was just the start. As Stop the War convenor Lindsey German recalls:

There were debates had and decisions made at every turn in the movement. Some people argued against us working with the Muslim community, some were against mass demonstrations and didn't like the fact that when we organised direct action, we tended to organise mass action with school strikes and so forth, some people wanted us just to protest at military bases rather than demonstrate.[101]

One of the first debates occurred at the first activist meeting. Some people wanted the new movement to adopt a complete programme, taking a position on a whole range of issues. The argument for focus won out:

We kept it very broad and very simple. We had three principles. Stop the War – obviously – defend civil liberties and resist racism. These last two turned out to be very prescient. But that is all people had to sign up to to get involved. Within that framework people could interpret the war in any way they wanted to, with a liberal view, a pacifist view, an anti-imperialist view, a socialist view or all of these.[102]

A little later at the first national conference some on the left argued that the movement had to take an explicit position against Muslim fundamentalism as well as against the US war. This call too was defeated. If it had not been, the movement would have been meeting the government halfway about the causes of the war. It would have softened and confused our arguments and demobilised the movement. Inevitably too it would have contributed towards the demonisation of all Muslim organisations that was taking place at the time. We had to focus on the Western powers, led by the US, not just because we were in the West, but because in reality they were the main driver of the war and the main source of the problems in the Middle East.

Taking this position was also crucial to one of the main sources of the movement's strength: the alliance with the Muslim communities. Most of the Muslim activists who came on board at the start were already political activists of one kind or another. The job was to reach out to the much wider layers of Muslims who were embittered by the war. As Andrew Murray, Stop the War's chair at the time explained, to do this meant breaking with some of the sectarian instincts of the left:

The November 2001 demonstration against the war on Afghanistan fell on Ramadan, the major Muslim holy festival. Thousands of Muslims wished to join the demonstration. To make that possible, however, some element of prayer would have to be incorporated into the final rally at Trafalgar Square, in order that pious Muslims could both protest against the war and maintain their religious observance. So that is what we did – an imam made the call to prayer at the appropriate moment and, after a brief interlude, the rally resumed. Of course this might not please secular sectarians, who would rather have a small rally than make any compromise to those feelings among the masses that they do not share. However, it was the right thing to do – it helped set in motion the alliance between the Muslim community and the left, which has enriched both since.[103]

The local and the national

Once the basic political approach had been agreed it was possible to create a national movement. National and local organisation reinforced each other. You can't have networked, co-ordinated local groups without a central point of organisation and you can't build a mass national organisation without local groups that can reach down into every part of society. Stop the War relied on different elements of the movement – socialist organisations, trade unionists, peace groups, Muslim organisations, anti-capitalists and lots and lots of new campaigners, just concerned citizens – to help put together a national network.

It helped that there was a formal agreement between Stop the War, the Muslim Association of Britain as it was then, and CND to co-organise the big demonstrations. But creating a movement on the ground also required tireless work on the part of a group of national speakers. Andrew Murray, John Rees, Lindsey German, Tariq Ali, Andrew Burgin, Bruce Kent, Jane Shallice, MPs George Galloway, Jeremy Corbyn, Alice Mahon and others travelled up and down the country for weeks between demonstrations, speaking at meeting after meeting. These public rallies and discussions were crucial in countering the mainstream media's narrative and popularising a series of arguments about the causes of the drive to war and the strategy for stopping it.

The idea of Stop the War groups caught people's imagination. They seemed to fit a need. Literally hundreds sprung up around the country, far too many for the under-resourced central office to keep track of, though the dynamic staff and volunteers did their best. By the time of the 15 February demonstration there were several local groups in many boroughs, let alone towns and cities, as well as groups springing up in colleges, schools and universities and some workplaces. Neighbourhood groups would have meetings of 50 or more regularly, and they were based around constant activity, leafleting, lobbying, postering, contacting the local unions and the media. It was these permanent and connected centres of radical opposition in communities up and down the country that produced such a remarkable series of massive mobilisations.

The international movement didn't emerge spontaneously either. The first suggestion for an international day of action was made at a 150-strong meeting in Barcelona in October 2002 that was planning for the European Social Forum scheduled for Florence that November.

British activists were already planning for the big demo in

February – so they suggested the idea of an international day. There was immediately some opposition. A number of key activists from the anti-globalisation movement felt that taking a position on war was outside the movement's remit and that it would threaten the unity that had been built up. The counter-argument put by the British activists present was that a movement that addressed economic issues and ignored war and imperialism would be impotent and irrelevant.

The debate became very heated; there were stand-up rows on the stage and the meeting nearly fell apart. After a tense debate, an agreement was made to work towards an international day and to make opposition to war a central element in the upcoming European Social Forum in Florence. The argument was vindicated. The main demonstration at Florence in early November effectively made opposition to war on Iraq its central theme. A million people came from all over the country to add to the 70,000 Europeans already there. In emotional scenes the great left-wing city became for one weekend an organising centre for European anti-imperialism. At an electric final rally in a disused railway station, 7,000 activists from all over the continent cheered and sang Italian partisan songs as the call was made for demonstrations to stop the war machine in every town and city around the continent.

At the end of the year another historic international gathering took place, this time in Cairo.

In Egypt too, different elements of the left and the movement were converging as a response to the gathering storm of war. Communists, radical socialists and some nationalists came together with some international delegates to convene the first meeting of what came to be called the Cairo Conference to try and develop the struggles against globalisation and imperialism. Egyptian activists already knew about the Stop the War Coalition and had been inspired by news of anti-imperialist resistance in Britain.

The day after the conference, 1,000 protesters gathered outside the Qatar Embassy in downtown Cairo to protest against Qatar's decision to allow US troops to be deployed on its soil. Though heavily outnumbered by troops, the protesters got away with it. One of those present, radical MP Hamdeen Sabahi, went on to march and speak at the 15 February demonstration in London, and the organisers went on to create the 'Tahrir Square Intifada' on 20 March 2003, the largest demonstration in Cairo for 20 years, and part of the inspiration for the Egyptian democracy movement.[104]

The word was spread in similar fashion at the 120,000-strong World Social Forum in Brazil at the end of January 2003. Again there were delegations and movement leaders who refused to talk about war, who regarded imperialism as being too divisive and difficult a subject to discuss in such a large movement. But anti-war activists pressed ahead and at one of the key rallies in a basketball stadium, where 20,000 people packed in to hear Noam Chomsky and Arundhati Roy speaking on the new imperialism, the call went up 'Don't attack Iraq' and the audience rose as one, fists in the air, recognising the war to be the key question that the movement had to respond to. Hundreds of demonstrations were hastily pulled together across Latin America and beyond, from that one weekend, just two weeks before 15 February.

Turning up the temperature

The majority of the millions who marched on 15 February hoped that a massive peaceful demonstration would make our leaders think again. As we will see, the demonstration very nearly tipped the balance against British participation in the invasion of Iraq. Any attempt to divert people to more militant action on the day would have led to a very small breakaway, summarily dealt with by the police. It would have broken the powerful sense of unity and allowed the police and the media to demonise a militant minority. But when on the Monday after the demonstration Blair continued his open defiance of public opinion, the energy of the movement turned towards more militant action.

In fact the sheer size of the demonstration meant the organisers had a platform from which to launch the biggest wave of direct action in British history. Two days after 15 February Stop the War launched a call for a nationwide campaign of direct action against the war. The national press could not ignore it. In an article in the *Guardian* headlined 'New protests planned to bring Britain to a standstill' Stop the War convenor Lindsey German was quoted calling on people "to walk out of their offices, strike, sit down, occupy buildings, demonstrate, and do whatever they think fit the moment war starts." She went on to say, "We want to completely close down Whitehall and prevent the Ministry of Defence going to work."[105]

Protests, sit-downs and most notably school student strikes started almost immediately, leading to a mass protest outside parliament on the day parliament voted for war. On 12 March Stop the War, along with CND and the Muslim Association of Britain, hosted a Peoples' Assembly in Methodist Central Hall in Westminster designed to represent the real opinion of the country in a way parliament was clearly failing to do. It brought together representatives of the anti-war movement from around the country but also people from the unions, political parties and community groups of all kinds. The assembly was addressed by MPs from Labour, the Liberal Democrats and Plaid Cymru, and by trade union and religious leaders. The Green Party also began to play a more central national role in the organisation. There were school students from Eton present with one of their masters, and there were speeches from a delegation of school students from Birmingham, as well as Billy Hayes, leader of the postal workers' union, CWU, and Bob Crow from the railworkers' union, RMT.

The atmosphere at the assembly was electric. Amongst many others, Bob Crow called for direct action and Billy Hayes urged as many CWU members as possible to get out in the streets, and called on the TUC to back action:

> When war breaks out we want to see as many CWU members as possible out on the streets protesting against this war... Isn't it time that the TUC said 'on the day war breaks out, every trade unionist should get in the street.'[106]

The assembly agreed to do everything possible to spread the slogan 'When war starts everything stops' and named a date for a day of school student strikes and occupations on 19 March.

Two days later, Stop the War sent out its most important e-circular ever. It was headlined 'Urgent...urgent...urgent... Stop work, college, school, the day that war breaks out.'

It called for mass stoppages and actions in cities around the country. It ended with a call from an RMT member saying "if they start a war, we must stop the country."[107]

This call was taken up around the country. As war approached, the movement was in a state of almost permanent mobilisation.

On the day the war started tens of thousands of school students poured onto the streets. At least 250 different workplaces struck, and thousands took direct action around the country. Many involved were taken by surprise at the scale of the action. Union press officer Trevor Phillips recalls:

> I was working in the HQ of the lecturers' union NATFHE. We were very supportive of the anti-war movement and I had a brief from the General Secretary Paul Mackney to give any support possible to people who wanted to take action. I had built up a network of people who pledged to do something, and on the day the war started I received mail from all over the country from people who were just walking out – often with their students – to show their disgust. I was astonished at

the scale of it, people in many, many dozens of colleges walked out. Some people issued statements, which were incredibly moving, saying why, as teachers, they felt they had a duty and a responsibility to show an example by taking action. It was an incredible feeling; I was flooded with messages for hours. And people were taking a risk. I suppose they took strength and courage from the popular mood and fact that two million had marched weeks before. It would have been a brave management who would have punished them. Also some were led by the students who in some cases just said we are not staying in our classes, you can come with us if you want to! I have always felt very privileged to have been in that position, it was a very inspiring and also very upsetting thing.[108]

Town and city centres around the country were closed by sit-down protests. The Mersey tunnel was blocked and the area around parliament in London was brought to a complete stand-still. In Leeds, 200 council workers walked out at just one office and joined hundreds more protesting in the city centre. All the main routes into the city centre were blockaded. Central Brighton was brought to a standstill by direct action involving more than a thousand people. Police used CS spray after protesters forced there way into the town hall. In Bristol over a thousand people, led by students from the City of Bristol College, confronted the police and ended up successfully blocking the M32 motorway. A rally in Piccadilly Square in Manchester drew over 5,000 people after students had poured out of Manchester Metropolitan University and blocked Oxford Road. In Cardiff the city centre was brought to a standstill as hundreds performed a die-in in the middle of the road. In Exeter 1,200 demonstrated and occupied the tax office, while school students occupied the main bridge over the River Exe.[109]

There is a myth that when the war started opposition melted

away. In fact the demonstration on 22 March, two days after the start of the war, was 500,000-strong, making it the biggest ever British march in wartime. After the war started there was a drop in those opposing the war. This was a temporary trend, however, and by November 2003 a majority opposed the occupation. This was no doubt influenced by both the failure to find weapons of mass destruction and the mayhem that the war was causing in Iraq. That month George Bush came to visit London and the anti-war movement came out once again in spectacular strength.

The police repeated the mistake of trying to ban the protest taking its chosen route – past Downing Street as Bush would be visiting the prime minister. They even threatened to close down the tube system. They made matters worse by blaming this demand on US homeland security. The prospect of the US security services telling people here where they could march didn't play well, and the negotiations over the route of the demonstration became a national news item. Days before the demo, the police caved in at a meeting at Scotland Yard, with TV crews crowding the entrance.

Despite a mini-media frenzy predicting violence and a serious terrorist attack in Istanbul killing several Britons the night before the demo, there was an enormous turnout of 300,000 – twice the number predicted and making it the biggest weekday demonstration in British history. The demonstration ended with the demolition of a huge statue of Bush constructed in sections out of chicken wire and metal foil by Norfolk-based group Artists Against the War. This was the movement's reply to the propaganda moment when Saddam Hussein's statue had been hauled down in Baghdad in front of the world's press. The difference was that there were many more cheering Bush's downfall in Trafalgar Square that night than there had been celebrating in the centre of Baghdad. The countdown to the toppling was called out by wheelchair-bound Vietnam veteran Ron Kovic, played by Tom Cruise in the Hollywood hit *Born on the Fourth of July*. That the 15-

metre statue crashed down inches from his wheelchair only increased the sense of tension.

Opinion hardened further against the war. The invasion had shattered Iraq's infrastructure and ripped apart its social fabric. It became obvious that the invading troops regarded all Iraqis as potential enemies and treated them as such. Thousands of civilians were killed or imprisoned and in some cases tortured, and by 2004 a good deal of Iraq was in open rebellion against the occupiers. The resulting repression and the sectarianism deliberately fomented by the occupiers led to the deaths of up to a million Iraqis. No wonder by 2007 some British polls were showing nearly 4 out of 5 people were against the war.

Historically large demonstrations over Iraq continued in Britain until the end of the occupation. A high point was one of Manchester's biggest ever demonstrations, when 50,000 confronted Blair at the Labour Party conference in 2006. And the movement that had come together against the wars in Afghanistan and Iraq extended to countering the wider project of the War on Terror. In 2006 Stop the War organised two emergency demonstrations against the Israeli invasion of Lebanon in two weeks, the second of which mobilised 100,000 after Tony Blair had expressed support for Israeli action.

When Gordon Brown took over from the disgraced Blair in 2007 he had little choice but to distance himself from Blair's Iraq policy. Just two months after becoming prime minister, Brown pulled the British troops out from their combat duties in Basra to the city's airbase. This retreat signalled an end to active operations. There was no attempt at triumphalism; the best Brown could do was insist, "This is not a defeat."[110] No one much believed him, but no one much cared. The point was the war on Iraq had become a humiliation and a liability.

Chapter Five

Blair on the Brink

"I thought: these really could be my last days in office."
Tony Blair.[111]

As war approached, Blair remained defiant in public. In reality, anti-war opinion and the anti-war movement nearly broke him. It caused consternation in government, the biggest backbench revolt in Labour's history, and very nearly forced Britain out of the Iraq invasion.

Later, Blair himself admitted to being isolated and desperate around the time of 15 February.

> The international community was split. UK public opinion was split. The party was split. I was between numerous rocks and innumerable hard places. The strain on everyone around me was almost unbearable. At home in Downing Street, I was a bit like a zombie...[112]

John Kampfner's account of the same period, based on insider interviews, confirms this picture. Blair was "shocked by the scale of the public hostility. Church leaders were speaking out. Former diplomats were speaking out. Labour MPs were signing motions in parliament, their confidence strengthened by safety in increasing numbers. It was around this time that the U.S. Embassy told the State Department that Blair was in considerable danger and needed support."[113]

The demonstration on 15 February was the moment of greatest isolation and stress for Blair and his coterie. They escaped London by travelling up to the Scottish Labour Party Conference where he was met with stony silence on the conference floor and an angry demonstration of 50,000 outside. One demonstrator recalls, "It was probably the biggest demonstration in Scotland since the 1920s, the atmosphere was unbelievable, from the size and from all the first timers you could see. We knew Scotland did not want this war, and so we were very loud and very determined."[114]

In the Blair camp the mood was dark. A close Blair aide confided, "This really was the moment of maximum pressure on him. As he travelled up there, we just didn't know whether the event would turn into a fiasco."[115]

Anti-war sentiment was so strong at this time, ministers were challenged when they ventured out in public. Alistair Campbell complained of loathing from people in the street returning from the demonstration as he was out jogging on 15 February.[116] David Blunkett was met with demonstrations and protests "everywhere" in his constituency, including at his constituency meetings.[117] Still he was shocked by the response he got at an *Any Questions* show at the end of February:

Everything was dominated by Iraq, and it was really hard work to win the audience round. The issue is obsessing everyone and permeating everything. It is affecting the world economy and creating a degree of insecurity and tension that everything else is feeding into.

Early in March, Tony Blair was verbally mauled on the *Tonight with Trevor McDonald* programme by the women studio guests, most of whom had lost a loved one in war or through terrorist attacks. They harried him with hostile questions and demanded that he called off British participation. Frustrated by his pitiful but obstinate response, they slow handclapped him as the credits rolled. As the normally sympathetic commentator Polly Toynbee spelt out, this looked like a government losing its grip:

It is a sign of sudden loss of authority that a programme could ambush the prime minister with not one word of complaint issued from Downing Street afterwards. Alistair Campbell was there in the next room watching this hiding-to-nothing on a monitor and saying not a word. Now it is open season and the prime minister was harpooned – again.[118]

Blair and his team weren't used to this kind of treatment. As two parliamentary votes on Iraq loomed, John Kampfner describes a state of virtual paralysis in Downing Street:

The British Government, in the normal sense of the word, had ground to a halt. A small group of cabinet ministers met several times a day. Hilary Armstrong the Chief Whip, and John Reid the Party Chairman spent their entire time trying to work out the extent of the forthcoming rebellion in the commons.[119]

It is clear that many in government circles thought the game was up for Blair. After France, Germany and Russia issued a joint statement distancing themselves from the US in early March, Blair recalled Jack Straw telling him that he was finished without a second resolution. Days later, the Cabinet Secretary Andrew Turnball was looking into what the Labour Party rules would mean for the government if Blair fell. Blair admits, "When I heard I laughed a little uneasily and I thought: these really could be my last days in office."[120]

Most significantly, an alternative to joining the invasion was being considered in the highest circles. Blair apparently told Piers Morgan it had been suggested by Bush himself: "When things got really hot for me politically here, and it looked like we wouldn't get the second UN resolution, Bush rang me and said: 'If you want us to go in alone, Tony, and join up later on, then we will do that. I understand your problems.'"[121]

Donald Rumsfeld's television appearance saying the US might go ahead without the British surprised Downing Street and made everyone very angry. It was interpreted as a pincer movement, an attempt to force the British to come out strongly and decisively in favour of war with or without a second resolution. But it also raised the possibility of backing out.

Senior Blair advisor David Manning and Jack Straw both argued strongly that the Rumsfeld statement had given Britain the opportunity to back out of the invasion and promise only humanitarian support down the line. According to Alistair Campbell's diaries, Jack Straw was adamant that Britain shouldn't be bounced into what was a US "war of choice," and that "some of these people around Bush could not care two fucks about us whatever, and that went for Tony Blair as much as the rest of us."[122] David Manning was arguing with anyone and everyone that getting Blair to agree to pull out of the invasion was the only way to save him. Few disagreed with him. Jonathan Powell seems to have been the only one who was really keen on the invasion. But in the cabinet, only Robin Cook and, briefly, Clare Short, broke ranks in public.[123]

Getting away with murder

When it came to the dramatic vote in parliament, the backbench revolt of 122 Labour MPs was regarded as just small enough to allow the government to go ahead. It was a close-run thing. Another 40 or so and Blair's position would have been untenable. Blair's success is often put down to his rhetorical brilliance and a series of persuasive speeches made to parliament, the Parliamentary Labour Party and the Scottish Labour Conference. This wasn't the case. Privately people remained unconvinced by Blair's arguments for war. David Miliband's view was that only about ten backbenchers really supported Tony Blair on this.[124] Political commentator Andy McSmith is certain that if there had been an honest and open cabinet debate followed by a vote, it would have come out against the war.[125]

There were two main reasons why this didn't happen. The first was the withered state of democracy in government. Blair famously didn't encourage collegiate government. Cabinet meetings were there to keep ministers up to speed and on message and involved little debate. When, on one of the rare moments in spring 2002, cabinet members dared to question Iraq policy and forced a serious discussion on it, Blair was incandescent. "A momentous occasion," wrote Robin Cook in his diary. Such authoritarian tendencies were made possible by the self-serving culture of careerism that permeated politics. In the words of Andy McSmith, "a habit of quiescence had developed in parliament and the cabinet in recent years, at least partly as a result of the massive increase in the number of ministerial posts. A concern for career and favour dominated."[126]

Even though many were uncomfortable and fearful about the war, challenging Blair seemed like too much of a personal and political risk. Clare Short, Minister for International Development, exhibited this survival instinct most publicly. After taking a critical stance on the war and calling Tony Blair reckless in a BBC radio interview, she threatened to resign from the cabinet if Britain went to war with Iraq without a clear UN mandate. Just days before the attack, however, she u-turned and announced that she would remain in the cabinet and vote for war because the prime minister had assured her she would have a lead role in post-invasion Iraq.

For many, this was a pivotal moment. In the words of Lindsey German, it was parliament that let the people down.

> Failure to stop the war was mainly due to the fact that a large number of Labour MPs went against the wishes of their constituents, as did many Tory MPs incidentally. If Clare Short had resigned, so soon after Robin Cook going, it might well have been impossible to continue. We now know how terrified

the cabinet were of the opposition, but failing an open challenge, the momentum of war just carried them along.[127]

But the war wasn't just a product of a poisoned political culture. As we have seen, opting out of the war or crossing the Bush government threw into question the centrepiece of British foreign policy – the 'special relationship' with Washington. Despite different interpretations and nuances, keeping close to Washington remains the beginning of wisdom for the whole of the foreign policy establishment in Britain. To do anything to challenge it raises the question of an alternative strategy. With the left in the Labour Party at an all time low ebb, and neoliberal dogma monopolising thinking in all parties, the possibility of forging a foreign policy based on anything else was beyond the imagination of the cabinet and most in parliament. Whatever their misgivings, few were prepared to face the intellectual challenge posed and the political isolation threatened by opposition. So the majority covered their ears to the public outcry, closed their eyes to the implications and voted for an illegal and catastrophic war.

Blair was not out of the woods though. We have seen how, after a downswing lasting a few months, opposition to the war started growing again from the summer of 2003. The huge demonstration during Bush's visit in November 2003 increased the pressure that was mounting anyway as the war proved both disastrous and deeply unpopular in Iraq. The Hutton Inquiry was a response to popular unease at the death of government scientist David Kelly, but it was also an attempt to deal with the single most glaring problem of the Iraq War – why, when Tony Blair had been insisting that there was clear evidence of weapons of mass destruction – had none been found? Lord Hutton's report was a whitewash, but the process itself, against the background of disastrous news coming from Iraq and continuing protest at home, became nearly intolerable for Blair.

In November 2003, Blair told Gordon Brown and Deputy Prime Minister John Prescott that he was planning to step down. He repeated the threat in a telephone call to the deputy prime minister in spring 2004. Baroness Morgan, the former director of government relations for Blair, confirmed he was in a mess at this time: "Iraq was a quicksand swallowing him up. The atrocities. Those terrible photos [of Abu Ghraib]. And he started losing people who had supported him throughout. He was stuck in this long dark tunnel and could see no way out of it."

He became so concerned about Iraq that he "spaced out" several times during parliamentary appearances and often woke up sweating in the night, it was claimed. It was only after persistent argument from his wife and close friends that he was persuaded to stay and stick it out.[128]

Though he managed to pull through this second war-related crisis, Blair never recovered from the collateral damage. Again and again he tried to "move the agenda on" from the war, but he never succeeded in recapturing the political initiative. In 2005 his huge majority was reduced to just 66 seats, largely as a result of anger over the war. Labour lost one million votes and suffered the shock of losing the symbolic Bethnal Green and Bow seat in London's East End to the Respect Party.

The moment when Blair's political demise became inevitable was in autumn 2006, soon after his announcement of support for the Israeli invasion of Lebanon. Stop the War organised two demonstrations against the Israeli action, surprising everyone by their size. Blair's former Secretary of State for Health, Frank Dobson, observed, "There were only three countries in the world against a ceasefire. Israel was one. The United States was another. And we were the third. People were nauseated."[129] On 5 September 2006, a letter signed by 17 Labour MPs called for Tony Blair to resign. On the same day, 49 other Labour MPs signed a statement supporting Blair's departure timetable. The next day, seven of the MPs who signed the letter resigned as Parliamentary

Private Secretaries.

On 7 September MPs challenged Blair on the Iraq War in parliament. Rumours about Blair's departure were circulating widely. A leaked Labour Party memo about strategies for Blair's exit from office called the Iraq War "the elephant in the room," which should be "incorporated into our media plan."[130] That same day he announced he would stand down within a year.

He couldn't disguise his crushing sense of isolation and disappointment in his resignation speech one year later. The war and opposition to it was a dominant theme.

Removing Saddam and his sons from power, as with removing the Taliban, was over with relative ease, but the blowback since, from global terrorism and those elements that support it, has been fierce and unrelenting and costly. And for many it simply isn't and can't be worth it. For me, I think we must see it through.[131]

Chapter Six

The Media in a Spin

"If you are going on the demonstration tomorrow, wrap up warm."
BBC One weatherman, 14 February 2003.

The protests against the Iraq War had a quite unexpected effect on the media. Most research suggests that the media tends to marginalise, ignore and even criminalise popular protest. This is so widely accepted that academics write of a media "protest paradigm," which includes framing protesters as variously violent, infantile, freakish, deviant or all of the above.[132]

Anti-war protests, with their implicit challenge to patriotic sentiment, seem to be particularly offensive to establishment journalism. Coverage of the protests against the first Gulf War in 1991 certainly fitted protest paradigm norms. *The Sun* columnist Richard Littlejohn ranted, "As the UN deadline passed, out crawled the usual collection of 'students,' Godbotherers, Guardian readers, gays, Communists, Trots, men with beards and duffle coats, men with ponytails, wimmin in men's shoes and old hippies with worn-out Country Joe And The Fish LPs."[133]

In his seminal study of the way the media responded to the new left and the anti-Vietnam war movement in the US, Todd Gitlin comes up with a list of typical knee-jerk media responses to mass protest:

- Trivialisation (making light of movement language, dress, age, style and goals);
- Polarisation (emphasising counter-demonstrations, and balancing the anti-war movement against ultra-right and neo-Nazi groups as equivalent 'extremists');
- Emphasis on internal dissension;

- Marginalisation (showing demonstrators to be deviant or unrepresentative);
- Disparagement by numbers (under-counting);
- Disparagement of the movement's effectiveness.[134]

It is a list that will be frustratingly familiar to most activists and recognisable to many occasional protesters. The protest paradigm can operate in a number of different ways. Marginalisation sometimes involves simply ignoring protest or relegating it to the inside pages. The *Guardian*, for example, had a policy of not reporting or giving prominence to demonstrations because they weren't regarded as newsworthy. This was a policy that only changed under popular pressure after the paper almost completely ignored the big demonstrations against the Afghan war – one of the first examples of anti-war protests changing media behaviour at the time. In general, coverage demeans protests, and its focus on the immediacy of the protest tends to downplay the issues that motivated it in the first place.

There were many examples of just this kind of behaviour over the Iraq War protests. The Murdoch press – all but one of whose 175 international titles were pro-war – did its best to ignore and then belittle the movement. Almost all of *The Sun*'s limited coverage of the protest was unfavourable. Next to none of it discussed the issues. But even *The Sun* was unable to dismiss the protests out of hand and unwilling to insult all those who participated. It had to grudgingly accept the scale of the protest and fell back on depicting ordinary marchers as dupes of hardened agitators. So on the Monday after 15 February at the same time as undercounting the demonstration, it ran the wonderful headline 'Demo led by usual suspects.' The same day's editorial congratulated the 58 million who didn't come on the march for not being "suckered by has-beens like Tony Benn and Michael Foot or never-will-be Charles Kennedy." In its editorial on 15 February the *Telegraph* too argued that the protesters were being naïve and thoughtless and showing no concern for the victims of 9/11.

Overall, however, the coverage of 15 February broke the mould. 15 February was not just widely reported on the front pages of the papers, most of them – excluding Murdoch outlets – cleared many pages to run features on it. The *Mirror* ran a 12-page 'souvenir supplement' to celebrate the demonstration. Other papers ran photo spreads, vox pops with marchers ('ordinary' and celebrity), and sent staff journalists onto the demonstration. Despite its editorial position, the *Telegraph* ran a four-page special with a photomontage of the demonstration on Monday, 17 February, featuring five interviews with participants entitled 'Why I marched' and one interview headlined 'Why I didn't march.' This last one, oddly, was an interview with Germaine Greer who expressed support for the protesters but apologised that she couldn't come because of a pressing deadline. The supplement also contained an eyewitness account by a reporter 'embedded' with protesters travelling from Diss and a global round up headlined 'Protest wave ripples round the world.' Meanwhile, BBC One ran twelve stories with a significant reference to the demonstration on its main evening bulletins in the days either side of the march.

Even more startling, the demonstration was hyped in advance across a wide spectrum of the media. Of the dailies, only *The Sun* and *The Times* failed to flag up the demonstration ahead of 15 February. Most provided maps, and all apart from *The Sun* reported on the organisers' (and sometimes the police's) prediction that it would be an unusually big demonstration. Two days before the demo, the *Daily Telegraph,* for example, ran a story headlined, 'Peace march could attract half a million.'

The *Mirror* actually campaigned for the demonstration with plugs by John Pilger and Hans Blix on 14 February and 15 February respectively, headlined 'John Pilger on why we should take to the streets tomorrow' and 'Blix gives us more reasons to join march.' The *Mirror* had been actively campaigning against the War on Terror since the end of 2001. As the movement grew its coverage became more and more confident and more and more linked to the protests. On 15 February the paper produced placards and banners for the demonstration.

After the sheer level of coverage, the most striking thing was its tone. Research into coverage in eight newspapers and on the BBC found that 46% of stories took a neutral approach to the demos, 28% took a favourable attitude to the protests and 7% actively promoted it. Only 41 items – about 19% – were "unfavourable."[135] The protest paradigm was at least partially suspended.

Feature writers from Euan Ferguson in the pro-war *Observer* to the *Mirror*'s Paul Routledge, the *Guardian*'s Madeline Bunting and the normally pro-Blair Jonathan Freedland, waxed lyrical about the power of protest. For Freedland: "Demonstrations have tremendous power. Their force grows rather than fades over time... The emotional experience of standing together in a shared cause serves as a political glue – it binds people into a movement. And it reveals the true state of public opinion more dramatically than any opinion poll ever could."[136]

In a piece called 'We are the people' Madeline Bunting wrote:

This was a day which confounded dozens of assumptions about our age... Saturday brought the entire business of a capital city to a glorious full-stop. Not a car or a bus moved in central London, the frenetic activities of shopping and spending halted across wide swathes of the city; the streets became one vast vibrant civic space for an expression of national solidarity. Furthermore, unlike previous occasions when crowds have gathered, this was not to mark some royal pageantry, but to articulate an unfamiliar British sentiment – one of democratic entitlement.[137]

Widespread coverage into the following week shows the media was not able to dismiss the demonstration as a routine protest. Directly counter to protest paradigm norms, it had to accept that the demonstration had played a crucial part in making Iraq into a crisis. By speaking of Blair's defiance of the demonstration on its Monday edition, the *Guardian* was investing the demonstration with the power to influence mainstream politics. More surprisingly, the *Telegraph* did the same in its Monday paper. Under the main headline 'Blair feels heat in war of words,' the subhead read, 'Iraq crisis threatens leadership, say backbenchers. Cabinet comes out fighting after huge march.' Later in the piece the authors quote Labour backbencher Alice Mahon urging the prime minister to think again:

> Any leader who attempted to take his people into war when there is this level of opposition would be making a huge mistake. It is difficult when leaders get themselves into this position where they do not have the support of the country. The wise thing to do would be to back off.[138]

A perfect storm

This unprecedented behaviour had a number of causes. For one thing, it reflected the fact that there were real divisions in the establishment over the war. As Seumas Milne argues, scepticism about the war extended way beyond the politicians, deep into the foreign office, the security services and even the military:

> There is no doubt that the government was panicked by the level of the opposition, particularly by the opposition within the middle classes. What was worrying to them was that these were not the usual suspects. This opposition was clearly spilling over into the political establishment; this was becoming an argument within the government. The Foreign Office was never really happy with the plans for war, and as it

came closer nor were whole sections of the political class. There were lots of stories that David Kelly was just one amongst a whole number of security people who were in semi-open rebellion. This was all partly a product of the demonstrations but it also gave confidence back to the movement and helped to legitimate it.[139]

Public opinion itself played a role; journalists and editors inevitably have to pay it some mind. Many papers were commissioning regular polls on the war and as we have seen the anti-war majority had been growing steadily since summer 2002. But the media are often only too happy to ignore opinion polls. The coverage itself attests to the fact that it was the scale and social weight of the demonstrations that was decisive. As one BBC producer explained, a demonstration of two million can't credibly be dismissed in the normal way:

> The knee-jerk option of ignoring it just isn't there. It's not politically sustainable, but anyway the impact of the demonstration seeps into the institutions. So many people have been on it that almost everyone knows someone who is there. You are in a different ball game.[140]

Leading Stop the War activist and press officer Andrew Burgin outlined how the scale of the movement and the stress on building new alliances impacted on middle class opinion, weakened establishment control over the media and challenged the idea that neutrality was necessarily a virtue:

> Though largely initiated by the left, it was so powerful that it wasn't a left-dominated movement. We managed to mobilise a huge breadth of social opinion, academics, show biz people, artists and so forth and this had an impact. The anti-war movement began to develop itself as a separate, recognisable

entity. People like Richard and Ruth Rodgers came on board, people who had been quite close to the Blair machine. And it all definitely had an impact on the media. Senior media figures sent us large sums of money, and the *Mirror* actually got in touch with us with a proposal. We went to meet them, they wanted to work with us, of course they kept their identity, but it was a kind of a breakthrough, this was unprecedented. It broke a taboo about media neutrality and the myth that the media was above politics, which is normally used to maintain distance from any kind of radical movement.[141]

Counter-reaction by media management and the Blairites attested to fear of anti-war opinion spreading in the media. At the *Observer* the editor and the political editor, who were both regularly lunching with Blair, refused to publish anti-war scoops and imposed a pro-war line without discussion even with senior editorial staff.[142] At the BBC, Director General Greg Dyke sent around a memo instructing senior editorial staff not to go on the demo and reminding them "they should remember their duty to be independent, impartial and honest."[143] Earlier, *Newsnight* management had sent around a memo decreeing that only moderate and pragmatic anti-war views should be mainstreamed on their programme.

Meanwhile Blair and his coterie had launched a "masochism tour" around the newsrooms of sceptical media outlets to try and win round doubters. If their experience at the *Independent* was anything to go by, the tour earned its nickname. Andy McSmith recalls:

Alistair Campbell took the whole editorial team out to dinner. Once we were in the restaurant he asked whether people supported the war. Every single person present indicated they were against the war except the proprietor and his wife. No one thought this hearts and minds operation was particularly well judged to put it mildly. People went along but it put their backs up.[144]

If the *Independent* editorial team didn't like being preached to by Alistair Campbell, journalists at the *Observer* were livid they hadn't been consulted about the *Observer*'s line and BBC staff were incensed by the ban on demonstrating.[145] The biggest single attempt at enforcing loyalty to government in the media was at the BBC, and it caused a serious crisis. It concerned the affair of David Kelly. Kelly was a government weapons expert who had suggested in secret interviews with BBC journalist Andrew Gilligan that the government had deliberately exaggerated the evidence for Saddam Hussein having weapons of mass destruction. Kelly's identity was eventually revealed and he was aggressively cross-examined at a parliamentary foreign affairs select committee. Two days later he was found dead, having apparently committed suicide. There is evidence that Blair sanctioned a strategy designed to reveal Kelly's identity.[146]

In the meantime, Gilligan was disciplined, not because the thrust of his story had been disproved, but because of minor inaccuracies. Later, Gilligan was called before the Hutton Inquiry that had been set up in August 2003 into the events leading up to Kelly's death. As the inquiry progressed the atmosphere in the BBC became threatening. According to Tony Lennon, the General Secretary of the Media union BECTU, a witch-hunt followed throughout the higher echelons of BBC editorial, particularly News and Current Affairs. There were literally dozens of disciplinary interviews in what Lennon describes as a "Spanish Inquisition."[147] All this caused resentment among staff, which erupted when the publication of the Hutton report in January 2004 led to the forced resignation of the BBC Director General Greg Dyke. In the words of a BBC worker:

The Kelly affair created a sense of crisis in the BBC. When

Greg Dyke came around after he was removed, he was cheered all around the building; it was a very emotional moment. Hundreds of people walked out of the building in protest responding to a call from journalist that cascaded through the building. Nothing like this had ever happened before. It was partly about the relationship between the government and the BBC which up to that time had appeared to be very good but suddenly had gone terribly wrong or at least was exposed as being very different from the one people thought existed. So this was about independence. It was also about the fact that the government appeared to have been caught lying and was now attacking the independence of the BBC as a way of protecting itself.[148]

Resuming normal service

These crude attempts to impose discipline in the media had mixed results at best. Coverage of the protests immediately after the war dropped dramatically but by the time of Bush's visit to London in November 2003 the movement was again attracting a lot of media interest. Despite attempts by the police to criminalise protesters in advance and politicians to patronise them as irresponsible and naïve, the protest dominated a good deal of the media for a few days. The *Telegraph* carried a map in advance and admitted the police had had to back down on their attempt to ban the demo from Whitehall. The images of Bush's statue toppling in Trafalgar Square were top item on TV news bulletins and the front page of some papers.

While some journalists bought into the police line about the dangers of violence, a lot of the coverage was sympathetic. A think piece in the *Mirror* argued 'The British are not anti-American... We just don't like Bush.'[149] The *Guardian* reported "by far the biggest turnout since the million-plus march in February; along with the crowds, the anger and conviction were back with a vengeance... Young and old, doctors, and teachers, students and the unemployed, representing every religion and every colour. They had come on foot and on bikes, by train and in cars."[150]

This positive coverage was partly a result of the fact that journalists felt the government had lied to them, and that, in the case of the BBC at least, the relationship between management and government wasn't what it should have been. As one BBC producer with the movement said of the press pack:

> Most of the time they are all in the Westminster bubble and they move together essentially responding to the official indications. When the spell breaks, however, another dynamic can emerge. I got the sense that there was anger at the fact they had been lied to over WMDs. I remember Radio Five Live broadcasting from outside the National Gallery in Trafalgar on the day Bush came, they had deliberately placed themselves with the protesters and they were doing loads of vox pops, just letting the people speak for themselves, and that meant effectively they were with the protesters. They weren't the only ones.[151]

In the months that followed, the government and media managements did force a return to normality. In a move that many compared with the ouster of Greg Dyke from the BBC, Piers Morgan was forced out as editor of the *Mirror* in May 2004, after the paper ran with what turned out to be fake photographs of British soldiers abusing Iraqi prisoners. His sacking was sudden and his treatment remarkable for such a senior figure. He was escorted out of the building without even being allowed to say goodbye to his staff. Two *Guardian* reporters wrote, "An atmosphere of fear has already descended on the *Mirror* newsroom, with normally voluble staff afraid to discuss the dramatic events. It is believed that there may yet be more casualties from today's meeting." They went on to quote one *Mirror* insider: "The government yet again have got their scalp and we went to war on a lie. There is a sense of a great misjustice here tonight."[152]

The level of coverage of the movement declined sharply. Despite very large protests by historical standards and growing opposition to the wars, the media effectively ignored the continued anti-war movement. By the time of the anniversary demonstration in March 2005, which attracted around 100,000 people, the media pack had moved on. Only a handful of papers reported it and then with a few column inches on the inside pages. The great demonstrations over Lebanon and Gaza received minimal media attention, and the BBC's pro-Israeli bias created such anger that one of the demonstrations in 2009 assembled at Broadcasting House to protest.

But for a few months in 2003 a mass movement had jammed the gears of the normally smoothly functioning media machine. The scale of the movement, the fact that it coincided with a moment of uncertainty within the establishment and the international isolation of Bush and Blair had all helped license dissent and even defiance of the official line. All this in turn had meant that anti-war sentiment had begun to affect the media itself. Protest had become normal, sensible even. At the time it didn't seem too odd that the BBC weatherman was recommending what to wear on the 15 February demonstration.

Perhaps above all else the movement's reception in the media can be put down to a sense that it had become a player, that it was influencing events. For Madeline Bunting, the media are interested in power above all. "If a demonstration looks like it might make a difference and have an impact, then it will become a focus of attention." At the start of 2003, there was a feeling in the air that people power might just have a part in shaping what suddenly looked like a very uncertain future.

On the day after the demonstration the *Telegraph*'s Matthew d'Ancona ended his comment piece with a warning: "Mr Blair now confronts a political vista outside his experience... And yet, to paraphrase Macbeth, if he should fail – well, then he courts unknowable political trauma."[153]

Chapter Seven

The Difference We Make

*"Q: Did News Corp. manage to shape the agenda on the war in Iraq?
A: No, I don't think so. We tried."*
Rupert Murdoch.[154]

The unfinished story of the anti-war movement attests to people's willingness to campaign on matters of principle, over issues that don't immediately or directly affect them, in their hundreds of thousands, and sometimes millions. Coming as part of a growing trend of protest, it challenges those who say people in the 21st century are disengaged, selfish, cynical or apolitical. And though the movement didn't stop the Iraq War, the panic in government, splits in the establishment and media turmoil it did help generate, all bear witness to the potential of mass protest in the modern world.

The power of the movement stems partly from the fact that its predictions have proved accurate, while the war leaders' assessments have been exposed as based on bravado, wishful thinking and bare-faced lies. We were told by the Pentagon's Ken Adelman that the invasion of Iraq would be a "cakewalk"[155] and by Dick Cheney that invading soldiers would be "welcomed as liberators."[156] Donald Rumsfeld insisted there was firm evidence of Saddam's weapons of mass destruction: "We know where they are. They're in the area around Tikrit and Baghdad and east, west, south and north somewhat."[157] John Reid, British Defence Secretary at the time of the first surge in Afghanistan, told the world he hoped that British soldiers would leave Afghanistan "without firing a single shot."[158]

As the movement's spokespeople warned it would, the invasion of Iraq turned into a savage war of occupation against a population that was in open and organised revolt in many parts of the country by the spring of 2004. The resistance forced occupation troops out of many important cities, including Fallujah and Najaf, and had overwhelming support amongst the Iraqi people by the middle of the decade.[159] The occupiers only contained the revolt by unleashing a toxic cocktail of violence and sectarian division that killed one million Iraqis and forced four million to flee their homes according to some of the most detailed research.[160]

Iraq's suffering is far from over. As well as continuing sectarian killings and chronic instability there is still a dreadful physical legacy. In 2012, US medical research in Fallujah provided a grim snapshot of the long-term damage done. Researchers discovered that due to increased exposure to depleted uranium, mercury and lead from bullets and shells amongst the population of Fallujah, there has been a "staggering rise" in birth defects since the war. In a place whose popular name has changed from "city of the mosques" to "polluted city," more than half of all babies are now born with birth defects.[161]

Many years and millions of British bullets since John Reid's comments, the Afghans are still under direct fire from Nato troops. In the face of the plain facts of growing opposition to the occupation and virtual social breakdown, even sympathetic commentators are starting to drop wilder claims about social progress, liberation and moves towards democracy. Under Western oversight Afghanistan has remained near bottom on UN development league tables, with "a level of deprivation similar to that found in famine zones" according to a 2012 UN-backed report.[162] Afghanistan is now the most dangerous country in the world for women.[163] Some still argue continued Western military engagement is necessary, but they ignore the facts and the history of the country. Far from being any kind of solution, foreign intervention is the prime cause of Afghanistan dysfunction over the last three decades and more. Once again, as the anti-war movement argued from the outset, Nato and Isaf operations in Afghanistan have made the region and the world a much more dangerous place and will leave a toxic legacy in the country. The sooner the troops go the sooner Afghans can set about dealing with it.

Hearts and minds

The movement's arguments have had a big impact on society in Britain and beyond. Despite a concerted campaign to get us to rally around the armed forces it is still the case that almost all opinion polls show big majorities against war policies. An autumn 2012 international poll on the US's standing in the world concluded that, "American influence on the world stage is being sapped by widespread distrust of US intentions" even amongst traditional European allies. It found that 40% of British people selected the word 'bullying' to describe American behaviour – more than in any other country or region of the world, and that only 12% of British people think that the US is defined by its respect for human rights. It also discovered that more British people opposed armed intervention in Syria than in any other Western country.[164]

Opposition to the war in Afghanistan has been above 75% in Britain for years now, and has only been kept in abeyance by the impression that the government is drawing down the operation.[165] As the human price of staying until 2014 has become clearer, opposition has hardened still; one 2012 poll found that fully four-fifths of the British population think that the war in Afghanistan has been a pointless waste of lives and money, and 52% think the troops should come out immediately and not on the government's timetable.[166] Even in the Libyan case, in which Western powers presented intervention as necessary support of a popular revolution, there was widespread opposition in Britain with polls showing a majority against the intervention for most of the period.[167]

No doubt the government insistence on the need for austerity and resulting cuts to welfare, wages and services has stoked opposition to costly foreign wars. But as we have seen, opposition has been constant or growing for many years. Focus group research in a detailed 2012 YouGov poll found that principled objection to Western intervention was widespread, with many participants believing that "Britain and the USA have no right to meddle in Middle Eastern affairs, and we should not be in these countries behaving like a colonial power, or trying to enforce democracy by military means on other cultures."[168]

One of the most important achievements of the anti-war movement has been to help popularise this kind of radical critique of Western foreign policy. This has included encouraging a historic shift in the way people understand the situation of the Palestinians. More people in Britain now believe the Israelis are a greater threat to regional peace than the Palestinians and believe too that the Palestinians should have their own state.[169] The scale of the demonstrations against Israel's attack on Gaza in 2009 revealed a widespread rejection of Western support for Israel's repression of the Palestinians. Supporters of Israel actually identify London as the epicentre of an international "red-green alliance" in support of the Palestinians, and they recognise that this support has come about "by allying with campaigns against the security crackdown following the events of 9/11 and British involvement in Iraq and Afghanistan."[170]

But it is not just that the movement has been able to shape opinion. Once mobilised, that opinion has influenced real events. We have seen how the movement helped force Blair out of office in disgrace over Iraq and ensured Brown had to be seen to change course. In the US, the anti-war argument and the movement behind it gave Obama the necessary impetus to take office. There was more continuity than change in Obama's foreign policy but his election was a set-back for the unilateralists.

More generally the movement has helped make war something that politicians regard as politically damaging rather than the election winner it was for Margaret Thatcher after the invasion of the Falklands in 1982. Without question this has slowed down and disorganised the warmongers. Insider discussions recognise that anti-war opinion in the US has been an inhibiting factor on any attack on Iran. As the editor at large of the influential *Foreign Policy* magazine put it, "The American people's war fatigue in the wake of Iraq and Afghanistan has made any complex, costly, or highly risky action a tough political sell back home."[171] Both presidential candidates in the run-up to the 2012 US elections played down plans for an attack on Iran. In Britain too, politicians register that post-Iraq, unilateral military action is much more difficult.[172] The British government's reported resistance to early co-operation in a US attack on Iran, on the grounds that advice from the attorney general suggested such an operation would be illegal, also reflects fear of the domestic political consequences.[173]

People and power

All this is important because it is all too easy to make poor political judgements on the basis of a sense of defeat. A good deal of the most influential radical critique of capitalism tends to emphasise the system's apparent ability to suppress conflict and to successfully mainstream elite ideas. Terry Eagleton notes that ever since the 1930s influential voices on the left have argued that society has become so bureaucratised and administered that "ideology, in short, is a totalitarian system which has managed and processed all social conflict out of existence."[174]

Similar conclusions were drawn by many after the disappointing outcome of the great social struggles that spread around the globe in the years after 1968. Michel Foucault, one of the most influential post-68 theorists of power, contended that power relations are so deeply inscribed into the very texture of our communication and interactions that most people can barely notice, let alone challenge them. These kinds of ideas still circulate widely. One contemporary critic influenced by Foucault argues the military industrial complex and the media form a seamless whole so powerful it almost inhabits us, operating as "an entire industry working together to produce the regime of official 'truth' and the popular conceptions, desires, fears and subjectivities which can enact and sustain it."[175]

Though no one has done more than Noam Chomsky to expose systemic bias in the media, particularly in times of war, his conception of media behaviour also leaves little room for challenge. He contends that, through a series of interlocking filter systems, "business-run thought control, to which vast resources and thought have been dedicated for many years" ensures that "media coverage keeps well within the bounds set by state-corporate power."[176]

Chomsky's "propaganda model," which so graphically explains the mechanisms by which pro-establishment bias is normally maintained, has been an aid to understanding the systemic nature of media bias, and the most popular radical alternative to liberal, pluralist models. But the predictions of the propaganda model don't account for moments when the ideological system runs into the problem of mobilised mass opposition. What is most interesting in the case of the last decade of imperial adventures is that the combined power of the Western governments, the military and the media have *failed* to win the argument for war.

Partly, as we have seen, this is a product of the context, the contrast between the US's economic decline and its military superiority, its consequent isolation in the world, its recent record of spearheading unpopular economic policies and so forth. Partly it is a product of the contradictions that exist within ruling ideas.

The impact of the anti-war protests show that the media

cannot be understood as existing outside of society. However much they may try, the ruling class cannot completely insulate the media from the struggles and experiences of the wider world. In fact, as media commentator Mike Wayne points out, the very ideology of neutrality and independence that sustains the media's role in normal times can become a problem for the elites when their behaviour becomes controversial. Of media producers he says, "objectivity, has, under the guise of working for all humanity, justified their role to capitalists, it has also inevitably led the intellectuals into conflict with their employers as and when the irrationality and partiality of capital has become too acute to ignore."[177]

But the scale and social weight of the anti-war movement has been decisive. The thousands of meetings and discussions around the country, the hundreds of outdoor rallies and street protests, the online information and debates, the confidence and solidarity generated by marching together, all these have combined to create a mighty ideological and practical challenge to imperialism which has yet to be rolled back.

The specific nature of the movement has also been important. Combining elements of traditional single issue campaigns with the generalised, radical politics of the anti-capitalist movement, rooted equally in the unions, the colleges and communities, and drawing together prominent intellectuals and writers with the radical left, the peace movement, the trade unions and the best of Labour, the anti-war movement has created something of a new model of organisation that has helped overcome the fragmentation of the left and the demoralisation of the labour movement.

When a movement becomes powerful and broad, when it coincides with and exploits divisions within the establishment, it has the potential not just to neutralise the mass media and win arguments, but to challenge governments. We are living in a world in which anti-war mobilisation has helped to weaken empire, and limited our rulers' room for manoeuvre.

Chapter Eight

Wounded Beasts

"As long as I am commander-in-chief we will sustain the strongest military the world has ever known."
Barack Obama.[178]

Since 9/11 US power has suffered a series of blows. The neo-con dream of a shock and awe-induced democratic surge is a distant memory. The war in Iraq that Donald Rumsfeld promised would be over in "five days or five months" lasted eight years. The Western powers made some material gains in Iraq, but their failure to achieve a decisive win and the sheer bitterness and attrition of the war has degraded their reputation as global purveyors of decisive physical force. Iran, the US's number one enemy – and half the reason for attacking Iraq in the first place – is now more influential in the region, not less. Even more humiliating, Iran now actually wields significant power in Iraq itself.

The outcome of the long war in Afghanistan looks as if it will be equally unhelpful to the champions of the Project for the New American Century. Despite Obama's conviction that Afghanistan was the "good," winnable war, the 2011 military surge has been a flop. Nato is still fighting over the towns and provinces it was contesting five years ago. The occupying forces express surprise at Afghan resilience. One British officer is on record complaining, "I am constantly amazed by them. They are completely over-matched by us and the Afghan army. We keep killing them, but they keep coming back for more."[179] But that is what people often do when their country is invaded and occupied. Unsurprisingly the Taliban appear to be growing in strength and support. Raids and insider attacks are becoming more audacious and the promised pullout can only embolden them. The condescending and frankly racist attitudes in much of the media will no doubt mean they will try and blame the abysmal state of Afghanistan on the Afghans themselves, rather than on the record of a savage occupation. But they won't be able to get away with it. The Afghan war will be remembered as both a military and security failure and as a humanitarian disaster.

If the War on Terror has been a chastening experience for US elites, triggering the return of mass protest as a constraining influence on US foreign policy, the news from elsewhere has not been much better. The left-leaning and virulently anti-US governments that have emerged in the US's Latin American 'backyard' over the last decade or so have proved extremely resilient. The Arab revolutions that have rolled out from Tunisia and Egypt directly challenged US hegemony in what it regards as the most important region of the world. Nothing could have exposed the emptiness of the West's democratic rhetoric more completely than Hilary Clinton's support for the murderous Mubarak dictatorship right up until the last possible, bloody moment. But those first two uprisings also illustrated the West's impotence in the face of mass movements committed to dealing decisively with their tormentors' and the West's allies. There was a heartening reciprocal logic at work here too, as the Egyptian movement, which had developed some of its early confidence from the global anti-war protests, delivered a knockout blow for democracy and a resounding defeat to Empire at the same time.

All this of course at a time of extreme strain for the neoliberal order. The international banking crisis has escalated into a crisis of state debt and of the state system in Europe, a crisis that threatens years of slump in the Western economies, accelerating relative economic decline. Underlying this many-sided crisis of US dominance is the rapid emergence of rivals, particularly, but not only, China as a world power. The refusal of Russia and China to endorse Western intervention in Syria at the United Nations serves as a symbol of their ability to challenge US power over central questions. As the neo-cons themselves warned it might, the unipolar moment proved to be short and not even particularly sweet for the US.

This serial humbling of the US, and by association its Western allies, can only be a welcome development. But we should be wary of thinking that it guarantees a return to some notional normality in international relations or the automatic ascendancy of moderate voices in the foreign policy debates in Washington, London or Paris.

Barack Obama was elected largely because he was perceived as being an opponent of the Bush Doctrine. Before the election he distanced himself from the rhetoric of the War on Terror, promised to close the Guantanamo Bay prison camp, to bring the troops home from Iraq and to improve the US's relationship with Iran and Cuba. He also committed himself to progress on the question of Palestine and to initiating a 'new beginning' in relations with the international Muslim community.

For a short time America's popularity in the Muslim world was given a boost by his election. But despite withdrawing the troops from Iraq, Obama's overall record on foreign policy has been poor. After repeatedly attacking Muslim countries with drone assassins, surging troop numbers in Afghanistan, failing to make any progress on Palestine or to close Guantanamo Bay, the US's standing in the Muslim world is lower than when Bush was in command.[180] Even the War on Terror rhetoric has been partially reinstated in briefings by administration officials seeking to provide a legal justification for the drone programme of targeted killing in Pakistan, Yemen and Somalia.

Obama's military budgeting indicates clearly that the US elites have not accepted a fundamentally less interventionist role in the world since the Bush years. His first defence budget for 2010 was $685 billion, 3% higher than in the previous year. He upped the ante again for 2011, requesting a total of $708.3 billion. In 2012 the president requested "only" $670.9 billion for the fiscal year 2012 – but the Department of Defense baseline request was actually raised from $548.9 billion to $553.1 billion. The overall decrease came only from an expected cut in operational costs for the wars in Afghanistan and Iraq. His projections allowed him to say in the run-up to the election that he is spending more than George Bush in real terms, and to brag that the US is continuing to spend as much on defence as the ten countries behind it in the league table.[181]

The problem is that, whatever the domestic political dynamic, the international situation facing the US president is an intensified version of the stressed scenario that brought us the War on Terror in the first place. The US remains by far the most heavily and effectively armed country in the world, while it is more and more challenged economically by emerging global and regional powers. US foreign policy debates recognise a shifting economic balance, but the question they consider remains the same: how to maintain US global dominance? Some emphasise the importance of soft power and "democratic ideals" in maintaining the US's position in the world, and the benefit of "co-operative multilateralism" in assuring hegemony.[182] But others focus much more on hard power solutions.

For these analysts the standoff over Syria symbolises not just a tipping balance of power but also the emergence of a direct conflict of interest with other emerging powers, especially China. In the words of Aaron L Friedberg, "What China's current leaders ultimately want – regional hegemony – is not something their counterparts in Washington are willing to give."[183] Friedberg, known as a realist rather than a hawk, goes on to argue that the US can respond effectively only by wielding military power in the region:

> In the absence of strong signals of continuing commitment and resolve from the United States, its friends may grow fearful of abandonment, perhaps eventually losing heart and

succumbing to the temptations of appeasement. To prevent them from doing so, Washington will have to do more than talk.[184]

This means recognising that Obama's efforts to toughen up China have been half-baked, and in practice "investing more in undersea warfare technologies, an area in which it already holds considerable advantages; deepening its co-operation with the navies of Australia, India and Japan among others; and supporting Southeast Asian nations' efforts to acquire weapons they need to defend their airspace and coastal waters."[185]

The view that the wind-down of the wars in Iraq and Afghanistan is coinciding with growing signs of confrontation between the big powers is widespread. In the words of Robert Fry, deputy commander of coalition forces in Iraq in 2006, "The economic challenge to the West, nuclear proliferation, cyber threats and the possibility of currency, water or energy wars all point to the return of great power politics."[186]

Although Obama has announced a re-focusing of foreign policy towards the Pacific region, the Middle East remains the centre of attention for the time being, as the Western powers and their competitors grapple with the fallout from the Iraq War and the challenge of the Arab revolutions. For mutually reinforcing energy and geopolitical reasons, the Middle East remains a non-negotiable part of the US sphere of interest, and though the US has been weakened in the area, it remains deeply embedded. The US counts Saudi Arabia and Israel, the region's most heavily armed countries, as its main allies; and it has several existing bases in Kuwait, in Saudi and the United Arab Emirates and new ones under construction in Qatar, Jordan, Oman and Bahrain, already home to the US Sixth Fleet.[187]

Surprise appears to be almost a permanent condition of the US political elites at present and they were as thrown by events in Tunis and Cairo as they were by the catastrophe at Lehman

Brothers two years earlier. But by March 2011 the US recovered sufficiently to develop a policy to try and contain the Arab uprisings. They adopted a two-part strategy. The first involved straight repression. Two days after US Secretary of State Robert Gates visited the island kingdom of Bahrain, an invading Saudi army joined local troops to brutally crush the Bahraini democracy movement.

The second approach involved attempting to appropriate the revolutionary dynamic through a military operation in support of the uprising in Libya. This, like the operation in Bahrain, had the support of Saudi Arabia and Qatar, but it was led by the US, Britain and France. The aim was not only to overthrow Colonel Gaddafi. It was also designed to buy the loyalty of the rebel forces by providing them with decisive military support.

Both approaches worked from the West's point of view, at least temporarily. The Bahraini movement was driven underground, and after some internal debate, the Libyan movement accepted Western help, with disastrous results. The best estimates are that the level of killing rose from 5,000 before the Western intervention to 50,000 by the time Gaddafi was killed.[188] In the process the country's infrastructure and political life has been blown to pieces. In the words of the International Crisis Group's North Africa Project Director at the time "The official optimism that masquerades as news these days assures us that Libya has been liberated and democracy is under construction there. But what is being constructed is a superstructure without a base... Libya today is a stateless country."[189]

In the case of Syria, elaborate efforts by the West to win over or discipline the opposition movement have dovetailed with the project of constructing a counter-revolutionary bloc centred on the Gulf States with the ultimate aim of isolating and crushing the Iranian regime. The indirect funding of, and engagement with, opposition groups by the US, France and Britain is widely reported. US allies Turkey, Saudi Arabia and Qatar have for long been both funding and as far as possible co-ordinating the opposition.[190]

Both opposition to direct intervention from China and Russia, and concerns about the unreliability of the rebel leaderships, have made the West hesitant about playing more than a co-ordinating and support role in what remains till now a proxy operation in Syria. But there can be little doubt about two things. First, even this limited intervention risks creating a regional conflagration. Second, that the Western powers are indeed signed up to a policy to try and ensure that a post-Assad regime is pro-West and pro-Israel, and that they see this as part of a wider plan to shatter what their allies in the region refer to as the "Shia Crescent," the supposed alliance of Hezbollah, Syria and, the West's main enemy in the region, Iran.

Understanding the interests driving the Western powers' current Middle East policy is vital because they are trying to use the Arab uprisings to repackage their interventions there as benign attempts to remove dictatorships and bolster democracy. Continued and unconditional Western support for the most unsavoury regimes in the region including Saudi Arabia, Yemen and Israel should make this rebranding difficult. But the West's efforts to co-opt the Syrian revolution has caused widespread confusion and it is noticeable how some liberal opinion has swung around once again to support the old idea of "humanitarian intervention."

Much has been made too of reported attempts by Nato powers to restrain Israel from attacking Iran. But any disagreements between Israel and its Western backers are about tactics and timing, not substance. The campaign to delay Israeli aggression has hinged on convincing the Israeli government that the US itself is going to get tough with Iran. In the words of one US official, "the key to holding back Israel is Israeli confidence that the US will deal with Iran when the moment is right."[191]

The US and Israel are anyway in permanent contact about the

options for joint actions against Iran. Reports suggest that plans are being laid for decisive, joint surgical strikes using bombers and drones. The insider rationale for such co-operation reads like a condensed exposition of US Middle East strategy. According to a source close to the discussions, the Israeli-led assault would be "transformative" and would end up "saving Iraq, Syria, Lebanon, reanimating the peace process, securing the [Persian] Gulf, sending an unequivocal message to Russia and China, and assuring American ascendancy in the region for a decade to come."[192]

Meanwhile, one effect of the War on Terror has been to spread instability southwards through Africa. Focused as it is on the Middle East and Pacific regions, the US is pressuring its Nato allies in Europe to take more responsibility for interventions in their old colonial stomping grounds on the African continent. Neither the French nor the British governments appear to need much persuasion.

The War on Terror has been a catastrophe for populations ranged on an arc from Central Asia to Africa. Thanks to resistance and domestic opposition, it has been a humiliating experience for the Western leaders who instigated it, including Tony Blair. But those leaders and their advisors are still at large and their policies have not been abandoned. "Secret" war plans, the increasingly savage sanctions against Iran, the accumulation of Western military hardware in the Gulf and the record arms sales to Gulf countries in the last year, are all pointing to the possibility of new wars in the region, while drone attacks and proxy wars are spreading.[193] As the pressures for war build, Western leaders are also no doubt pondering the downsides and the difficulties. The record of the years since 9/11 will ensure that domestic political reaction will be one of them.

In the words of Sabah Jawad, an Iraqi anti-war activist and political exile from Saddam Hussein's Iraq:

The Iraqi people were amazed at the level of support they had from Britain. The anti-war movement clearly inflicted heavy damage on the Labour government and on the policy they pursued. The decision-makers that took Britain into the war are discredited; Blair can't even go out onto the streets in Britain without facing public outcry. Any government will find it much more difficult to pursue these kinds of plans in the future, but we have to be ready to go out into the streets once again because the West's leaders are like wounded beasts, and they are still hungry for power.[194]

Endnotes

1. Campbell, A. (2012) *The Burden of Power: Countdown to Iraq*, p.490
2. Blair, T. (2010) *A Journey*, p.429
3. Campbell, A. (2012) *The Burden of Power: Countdown to Iraq*, p.491
4. Wintour, P., *The Guardian* 26 April 2003, 'Blair's road to war: Brought to the brink of defeat.'
5. As above.
6. Tyler, P. E., *New York Times*, 17 February 2003, 'Threats and responses: news analysis; a new power in the streets.' Available at: http://www.nytimes.com/2003/02/17/world/threats-and-responses-news-analysis-a-new-power-in-the-streets.html
7. Blair, T. (2010) *A Journey*, p.414
8. Campbell, A. (2012) *The Burden of Power: Countdown to Iraq*, p.460
9. Randeep, R. (ed) (2003) *The War We Could Not Stop: The Real Story of the Battle for Iraq*, pp.70-73
10. Davies, N. (2008) *Flat Earth News*, p.396
11. Quoted in Wintour, P., *The Guardian* 26 April 2003, 'When Blair stood on the brink.'
12. Woodward, B. (2002) *Bush at War*, pp.83 and 91
13. Lemann, N., *The New Yorker*, 1 April 2002. 'The Next World Order: The Bush Administration may have a brand-new doctrine of power.'
14. Callinicos, A. (2003) *The New Mandarins of American Power*, p.51
15. Frum, D. (2003) *The Right Man*, p.196
16. Kessler, G., *Washington Post*, 12 January 2003, 'US decision on Iraq has puzzling past.'
17. *ABC News* 30 January 2002, 'Bush Delivers State of the Union

Address.' Available at: http://abcnews.go.com/Politics/story ?id=121225&page=1#.UJBThBi6Dbl

18. Murphy, C. and Purdum, T., *Vanity Fair* February 2009, 'Farewell to all that: An Oral History of the White House.' Available at: http://www.vanityfair.com/politics/features/20 09/02/bush-oral-history200902

19. Rawnsley, A. (2010) *The End of the Party: The Rise and Fall of New Labour*, p.83

20. Memo from Manning to Blair, 14 March 2002, quoted in Rawnsley A., p.87. Available at: http://downingstreetmemo .com/meyertext.html

21. Confidential and Personal Letter from Meyer to Manning, 18 March 2002. Quoted in Rawnsley A., p.87

22. Kampfner, J., (2003) *Blair's Wars*, p.167

23. Rawnsley, A. (2010) *The End of the Party: The Rise and Fall of New Labour*, pp.96-7

24. As above, p.96

25. Kampfner, J. (2003) *Blair's Wars*, p.167

26. Le Carre, J. (2006) 'The United States has Gone Mad.' In *Not One More Death*, pp.9-10

27. Kumar, D. (2012) *Islamophobia and the Politics of Empire*, p.113

28. Gardner, L. C. (2008) *The Long Road to Baghdad: A History of US Foreign Policy from the 1970s to the Present*, p.63-4

29. See notably Anderson, P, 'Jottings on the Conjuncture.' In *New Left Review*, November-December 2007, pp.12-13

30. Hardt, M. and Negri, A. (2000) *Empire*, and (2004) *Multitude: War and Democracy in the Age of Empire*.

31. See for example, Panitch, L. and Gindin, S. (2005) 'Finance and American Empire.' In *Socialist Register* 2005, pp.46-81

32. Quoted in Harvey, D. (2007) 'Neoliberalism as Creative Destruction.' In *The ANALS of the American Academy of Political and Social Science*, p.610

33. Suskind, R. T., *New York Times Magazine* 17 October 2004, 'Faith, Certainty and the Presidency of George W. Bush.'

34. 'Rebuilding America's Defenses: Strategy, Forces and Resources For a New Century.' In *A Report of The Project for the New American Century*. Available at: www.newamrican-century.org

35. Rees, J. (2006) *Imperialism and Resistance*, p.42

36. Harvey, D. (2003) *The New Imperialism*, p.62

37. Rees, J. (2006) *Imperialism and Resistance*, p.59

38. As above, p.14

39. As above, p.30

40. Blair, T. (2010) *A Journey*, p.388

41. Blair, T. (1999) 'Doctrine of the International Community,' Speech to the Economic Club, Chicago, 24 April 1999. Available at: http://homepages.warwick.ac.uk/~poseaj/380/380/documents/speeches1.html

42. Cooper, R. (2001) 'The Next Empire,' *Prospect*, 20 October 2001

43. Rawnsley, A. (2010) *The End of the Party: The Rise and Fall of New Labour*, p.92

44. Kampfner, J. (2003) *Blair's Wars*, p.216

45. Rawnsley, A. (2010) *The End of the Party: The Rise and Fall of New Labour*, p.157

46. Filkins, D., *The New York Times*, 7 December 2003 'A Region Inflamed: Tough New Tactics by US Tighten Grip on Iraq Towns.'

47. Quoted in Zinn, H. (2011) *On War*, p.121

48. Solomon, N. (2005) *War Made Easy*, p.237

49. See for example, Knightley, P. (1975) *The First Casualty*

50. Cited by Foster 1992, p.158

51. Wells, T. (1994) *The War Within*, p.428

52. CBS poll, 23 January, 2003. Available at: http://www.cbsnews.com/stories/2003/01/23/opinion/polls/main537739.shtml

53. Rees, J. (2006) *Imperialism and Resistance*, p.54

54. As above, p.55

55. Kagan, R. (2003) *Paradise and Power: America and Europe in the New World Order*, p.37

56. Project for the New American Century Report, 2000.

57. Kumar, Deepa, (2012) *Islamophobia and the Politics of Empire*, p.114

58. Fekete, L. (2009) *A Suitable Enemy*, p.103

59. See for example Fekete, L. (2009) *A Suitable Enemy*, particularly Chapter 4

60. See for example, Steele, J. (2011) *Ghosts of Afghanistan*

61. See for example *UN News Centre*, 7 March 2003, 'Blix welcomes accelerated cooperation by Iraq, but says unresolved issues remain.' Available at: http://www.un.org/apps/news/story.asp?NewsID=6383&Cr=iraq&Cr1=inspect#.UGcuNRisPbk

62. Ensor, D., *CNN*, 15 March 2003, 'Fake Iraq documents "embarrassing" for US.' Available at: http://edition.cnn.com/2003/US/03/14/sprj.irq.documents/

63. 'Iraq's Weapons of Mass Destruction: The Assessment of the British Government' 24 September 2002. Available at: http://www.archive2.official-documents.co.uk/document/reps/iraq/cover.htm

64. Sparrow, A., *The Guardian*, 8 December 2009, '45-minute WMD claim "may have come from an Iraqi taxi driver."'

65. Pascoe-Watson, G., *The Sun* 25 September 2002, 'Brits 45 Mins from Doom' and *Evening Standard* 24 September 2002, '45 Minutes from Attack.'

66. Klandermans, B. (2010) 'Peace Demonstrations or Anti-government Marches?' In Walgrave and Rucht (eds) *The World Says No to War*, p.100

67. Chomsky, N. and Achcar, G. (2007) *Perilous power: The Middle East and US Foreign Policy*, p.43

68. Rohde, D., *New York Times*, 19 June, 2003, 'Iraqis Were Set to Vote, but US Wielded a Veto.' Available at: http://www.nytimes.com/2003/06/19/international/worldspecial/19NAJ

A.html
69. Quoted in Harvey, D. (2003) *The New Imperialism*, p.214
70. Armstrong, D. (2002) Dick Cheney's song of America, *Harper's Magazine*, October 2002, Vol. 305, Issue 1829. Available at: http://www.informationclearinghouse.info/art icle1544.htm
71. Tyler, P., *The New York Times*, 17 February 2003, 'A New Power In the Streets.'
72. Walgrave, S. and Rucht D. (2010) 'Demonstrations against the War on Iraq', p.1 and Seppala T. (2010) *Globalizing Resistance Against War?* p.1
73. *Socialist Worker*, 22 February 2003, 'The day the world said no to war on Iraq'
74. Reported on GSOA website http://www.gsoa.ch/themen /krieg-und-frieden/
75. Chan, S., *CBS News*, 11 February 2009, 'Massive Anti-War Outpouring.' Available at: http://www.cbsnews.com/2100-500257_162-540782.html
76. Vidal, J., *The Guardian* 13 February 2003, '10 million join world protest rallies.'
77. *The World Says No to War*, Larry Neilson, Director's Cut, 15 February 2003. Available at: http://www.cityofart.net /movies/worldsaysno.html
78. *CNN News*, 15 February 2003, 'US Sees Protests Big and Small.'
79. Leupp, G., *Counterpunch* 25 February 2003, 'Notes on the Numbers'
80. *Socialist Worker*, 22 February 2003, 'The day the world said no to war on Iraq.'
81. Numbers discussed in detail in Murray, A. and German, L. (2005), *Stop the War, The Story of Britain's Biggest Mass Movement*, p.163
82. Jenny Johnston quoted in *The Daily Mirror*, 17 February 2003
83. Mike Shaw interviewed in *The Guardian*, 17 February 2003

84. Williams, R., *The Guardian*, 17 February 2003, 'Flood of emotion and anger that rose to wash away years of dismay.'

85. Bunting, M., *The Guardian*, 17 February 2003, 'We are the people.'

86. Walgrave, S. Rucht, D. and Van Aelst, P. (2010) 'New Activists or Old Leftists?' In Walgrave, S and Rucht, D (2010), p.87.

87. Della Porta, D. (2010) in Walgrave, S. and Rucht, D. (2010), p.127

88. British Social Attitudes Survey, quoted in Cousins, A. *Counterfire*, 27 November 2011, 'The Crisis of the British Regime: Democracy, Protest and the Unions' Available at: http://www.counterfire.org/index.php/theory/37-theory/ 14906-the-crisis-of-the-british-regime-democracy-protest- and-the-unions

89. World Values Survey quoted in Cousins, A., as above

90. As above.

91. Figures quoted in Cousins, A., as above

92. As above.

93. As above.

94. As above.

95. As above.

96. Interview by author with Lindsey German, 31 October 2012

97. Rees, J. (2006), *Imperialism and Resistance*, p.222-3

98. Shaheda Vawda interviewed in *War. Anti-War,* a film by Tansy Hoskins and John Rees for the Islam Channel, September 2011

99. John Rees interviewed in *War. Anti-War*

100. Jeremy Corbyn MP interviewed in *War. Anti-War*

101. Interview by author with Lindsey German, 31 October 2012

102. Andrew Murray interviewed in *War. Anti-War*

103. Murray, A. and German, L. (2005) *Stop the War: The Story of Britain's Biggest Mass Movement*, p.62

104. Rees, J. (2005) 'Cairo Calling.' In Murray, A. and German, L.,

Stop the War, The Story of Britain's Biggest Mass Movement,
p.209-210

105. Vidal, J., Wilson, J. and Branigan, T., *The Guardian* 17
February 2003, 'New protests planned in bid to Britain to a
standstill.'

106. Bishopsgate Institute, Stop the War archive, 17 March 2003

107. As above.

108. Interview by author with Trevor Phillips, 2 October 2012

109. Reports taken from 'A Country in Revolt.' In Murray, A. and
German, L. (2005) *Stop the War, The Story of Britain's Biggest
Mass Movement,* p.191-196

110. Batty, D., *The Guardian* 3 September 2007, 'British forces
complete withdrawal from Basra.'

111. Blair, T. (2010) *A Journey,* p.429

112. As above, p.424

113. Kampfner, J. (2003) *Blair's Wars,* p.274

114. Interview by author with Joan Humphries, 7 October 2012

115. *Financial Times,* 29 May 2003, p.17

116. Campbell, A. (2012) *The Alastair Campbell Diaries,* Vol 4,
p.460

117. Blunkett, D. (2006) *The Blunkett Tapes,* p.466

118. Toynbee, P. *The Guardian,* 12 March 2003

119. Kampfner, J. (2003) *Blair's Wars,* p.29

120. Blair, T. (2010) *A Journey,* p.429

121. Morgan, P. (2005) *The Insider,* p.456

122. Campbell, A. (2012) *The Alastair Campbell Diaries,* p.492

123. As above, p.492

124. As above, p.469

125. Interview by author with Andy McSmith, 22 June 2011

126. As above.

127. Interview by author with Lindsey German, 31 October 2012

128. Winnett, R. *The Daily Telegraph,* 1 March 2010, 'Tony Blair
"considered resigning in wake of Iraq war."'

129. Rawnsley, A. (2010) *The End of the Party: The Rise and Fall of*

New Labour, p.385

130. Aparnaa, S., *ABC News*, 7 September 2006, 'Tony Blair to Resign in a Year.'
131. Wintour, P. and Woodward, W., *The Guardian*, 11 May 2007, 'I did what I thought was right.'
132. See for example Mcleod, D.M. and Hertog, J.K. (1999) 'Social Control and the Mass Media's role in the Regulation of Protest Groups: The Communicative Acts Perspective.' In Demers, D and Viswanath, K. (eds) *Mass Media, Social Control and Social Change*, pp.305-330
133. Quoted in Wilcox, D. R. (2005) *Propaganda, the Press and Conflict: the Gulf War and Kosovo*, p.142.
134. Gitlin, T. (1980) *The Whole World is Watching: Mass Media in the Making and Unmaking of the New Left*
135. Based on my ongoing research at University of Westminster's Communication and Media Research Institute. Results to be published in 2013.
136. Freedland. J., *The Guardian* 17 February 2003, 'Marchers have the power to make a difference.'
137. Bunting, M., *The Guardian* 17 February 2003, 'We Are the People.'
138. Helm, T., *Daily Telegraph* 17 February 2003, 'Blair feels the heat in war of words.'
139. Interview by author with Seumas Milne, 26 May 2011
140. Interview by author with Iain Bruce, 11 May 2012
141. Interview by author with Andrew Burgin, 28 May 2011
142. Interview by author with Ed Vulliamy, 17 May 2012
143. Quoted in Deans, J., *The Guardian* 11 February 2003, 'BBC bans news stars from anti-war march.'
144. Interview by author with Andy McSmith, 22 June 2011
145. Interviews by author with Ed Vulliamy and Iain Bruce
146. Rawnsley, A. (2010) *The End of the Party: The Rise and Fall of New Labour*, p.211
147. Interview by author with Tony Lennon, 1 August 2012

148. Interview by author with Paul Alexander, 26 June 2011

149. Freedland, J., *The Guardian*, 17 November 2003, 'The British are not anti-American, we just don't like Bush.'

150. Wilson, J. and Taylor, M., *The Guardian* 21 November 2003, 'And down comes the statue... but this time it's Trafalgar Square.'

151. Interview by author with Niall Sookoo, 14 August 2011

152. Tryhorn, C. and O'Carroll, L., *The Guardian*, 14 May 2004, 'Morgan sacked from Daily Mirror.'

153. D'Ancona, M., *Sunday Telegraph* 16 February 2003

154. Davies, N., *The Guardian*, 25 April 2012, 'The questions Rupert Murdoch must answer at the Leveson inquiry.'

155. Adelman, K., *Washington Post*, 13 February 2002, 'Cakewalk in Iraq'

156. Meet the Press *NBC News* 14, September 2003. Available at: http://www.msnbc.msn.com/id/3080244/ns/meet_the_press/t/transcript-sept/#.UJF2yRi6Dbk

157. *ABC News* 30 March 2003

158. Quoted in Harding, T., *Daily Telegraph*, 12 January 2008, 'A year in Helmand: 4m bullets fired by British.'

159. Milne, S. (2012) *The Revenge of History*, p.121

160. The death toll in Iraq is controversial and difficult to gauge as the US made the conscious decision not to assess Iraqi casualties. The figures given here are based on a study led by researchers from Johns Hopkins University in Baltimore and published in the prominent British journal The Lancet Burnham, G., Lafta, R., Doocy, S., and Roberts, L. (2006) Mortality after the 2003 invasion of Iraq: a cross-sectional cluster sample survey, *The Lancet*, volume 368, issue 9545, pp.1421-1428.

For a useful summary of the debates about the numbers of dead in Iraq see Steele, J and Goldenberg, S., *The Guardian* 19 March 2008, 'What is the Real Death Toll in Iraq?'

161. Morrison, S., *Independent on Sunday*, 14 October 2012, 'New

report shows huge rise in birth defects due to US bombing of Iraq.'

162. Graham-Harrison, E., *The Guardian,* 4 September 2012, 'Prevalence of malnutrition in southern Afghanistan "shocking" in Kandahar.'

163. Global Perceptions Survey, June 2012, carried out by TrustLaw, the Thomson Reuters Foundation's legal news service. Available at: www.trust.org/trustlaw. Summary available at http://uk.reuters.com/article/2011/06/15/uk-women-dangerfbidUKTRE75E0D520110615

164. YouGov international survey taken between 10 and 25 August, 2012, summarised in Borger, J. and Clark, T., *The Guardian* 12 September 2012, 'US lacks world's trust, poll finds.'

165. See for example Prince, R., *Daily Telegraph* 18 April 2010, 'General election 2010: war in Afghanistan to play part UK in campaign.' The Com Res poll reported found that 77% wanted troops to be withdrawn from Afghanistan, while more than half thought that the presence of troops there put British streets at greater risk from terrorism.

166. Lyons, J., *Daily Mirror,* 24 September 2012, 'Get our heroes out of pointless Afghan war now Mirror poll finds.' Available at: http://www.mirror.co.uk/news/uk-news/britons-want-troops-to-quit-afghanistan-1340733

167. See for example, YouGov poll, 6 April 2011, 'YouGov show public turning against Libya bombing.' Available at: http://ukpollingreport.co.uk/blog/archives/3412

168. See MacLeod, H., *YouGov Politics Lab* 23 May 2005. Afghanistan: should we stay or should we go? Available at: http://yougov.co.uk/news/2012/05/23/afghanistan-should-we-stay-or-should-we-go/

169. Abdullah, D. and Chehata, H. (2012) European Public Perceptions of the Israel-Palestine Conflict: An analysis of a European survey carried out by ICM for Aljazeera Center

for Studies, the Middle East Monitor and the European Muslim Research Centre

170. Bright, M, *The Jewish Chronicle* 29 December 2010, 'Britain leads in Israeli denial efforts.'

171. Rothkopf, D. (2012) 'A Truly Credible Threat to Iran,' *Foreign Policy* 8 October 2012

172. See for example Paddy Ashdown's appearance on *The BBC Politics Show* 12 June 2012. Available at: http://www.bbc.co.uk/news/uk-politics-18410124

173. Hopkins, N., *The Guardian* 25 October 2012 'Britain rejects US request to use UK bases in nuclear standoff with Iran.'

174. Eagleton, T. (1991) *Ideology: An Introduction*, p.127

175. Jayyusi, L. (2011) 'Terror, War and Disjuncture in the Global Order in Freedman D. and Thussu, D.' *Media and Terrorism*, p.40.

176. Chomsky, N. (1994) *World orders Old and New*, pp.88-91

177. Wayne, M. (2003) *Marxism and Media Studies: Key Concepts and Contemporary Trends*, pp.23-24

178. Speech in San Francisco, 9 October 2012. Available at: http://www.telegraph.co.uk/news/worldnews/us-election/9597443/US-Election-2012-President-Barack-Obama-defends-his-foreign-policy.html

179. Hopkins, N., *The Guardian,* 20 September 2012, 'Battle inside Afghanistan's most violent corner in Nahr-e Saraj.'

180. Smith, J.A., *Counterpunch,* 16 October 2012, 'Obama's War Record.'

181. Sahadi, J., *CNN Money,* 18 October 2012, 'Defense: $2 trillion divides Obama and Romney.'

182. See for example Haas, R. N. (2008) 'The Age of Nonpolarity: What Will Follow US Dominance,' *Foreign Affairs*, May/June 2008, pp.44-56 and Zakaria F. (2008) 'Is America in Decline? Why the United States Will Survive the Rise of the Rest?,' *Foreign Affairs*, May/June 2008, p.18-43

183. Friedberg, A. L. (2012) Bucking Beijing, *Foreign Affairs*,

September/October 2012, p.50

184. As above, p.53
185. As above, p.55
186. Fry, R. (2012) Survival of the Fittest, *Prospect,* November 2012, p.29-34
187. See map of Middle East bases in Rees, J., *Counterfire,* 1 August 2012, 'Empire and revolution – Syria and the critics of the anti-war movement.'
188. Milne, S., *The Guardian* 26 October, 2012, 'If the Libyan war was about saving lives, it was a catastrophic failure.'
189. Roberts, H., *London Review of Books,* 11 October, 2012, 'Western Recklessness' p.27
190. See for example Borger, J., *The Guardian,* 14 August, 2012, 'Syria crisis: West loses faith in SNC to unite opposition groups.' For a collection of other sources see http://shashankjoshi.wordpress.com/2012/07/28/the-not-so-secret-war-in-syria/
191. Wintour, P. and Hopkins, N. *The Guardian,* 26 October 2012, 'Iran military action not "right course at this time", Downing Street says.'
192. Wrenn, E., *The Daily Mail* 9 October 2012, 'US and Israel "considering joint aerial strike" against Iran's nuclear facilities using bombers and drones.'
193. Shanker, T., *New York* Times, 27 August 2012, 'United States arms sales triple: preparing for war with Iran.'
194. Interview by author with Sabah Jawad, 2 November 2003

Contemporary culture has eliminated both the concept of the public and the figure of the intellectual. Former public spaces – both physical and cultural – are now either derelict or colonized by advertising. A cretinous anti-intellectualism presides, cheerled by expensively educated hacks in the pay of multinational corporations who reassure their bored readers that there is no need to rouse themselves from their interpassive stupor. The informal censorship internalized and propagated by the cultural workers of late capitalism generates a banal conformity that the propaganda chiefs of Stalinism could only ever have dreamt of imposing. Zer0 Books knows that another kind of discourse – intellectual without being academic, popular without being populist – is not only possible: it is already flourishing, in the regions beyond the striplit malls of so-called mass media and the neurotically bureaucratic halls of the academy. Zer0 is committed to the idea of publishing as a making public of the intellectual. It is convinced that in the unthinking, blandly consensual culture in which we live, critical and engaged theoretical reflection is more important than ever before.